"Trabert provides a superbly researched account of the fiscal battles that have engulfed Kansas government in recent years. Recent tax cuts in other states were successful, but Gov. Brownback's tax reforms created major blowback. Trabert's story will be interesting reading for anyone who follows state politics."

—Chris Edwards, Director,
Tax Policy Studies, Cato Institute

"The Left always has an excuse to oppose tax cuts, but the reason is always the same: they want more of your money. This book provides reasoned analysis and insight into the real story behind the Kansas tax cuts and what other states can truly learn from what happened in Kansas."

—Tim Huelskamp, PhD, President,
The Heartland Institute

"*What Was* Really *the Matter with the Kansas Tax Plan* is a refreshingly candid examination of _____ opportunities and the disingenuous attem_____ interests to discourage tax relief. Ind_____ cut taxes, and other states can do s_____ ing the lessons learned in Kansa_____

_____ Buck,
_____ Senator,
_____ al Chair of
American Legislative _____ ange Council

What Was *Really* the Matter with the Kansas Tax Plan

The Undoing of a Good Idea

What Was *Really* the Matter with the Kansas Tax Plan

The Undoing of a Good Idea

By Dave Trabert

with Danedri Herbert

JAMESON BOOKS, INC.
Ottawa, Illinois

Contents

Foreword

by Former US Senator Tom Coburn, MD

"The first lesson of economics is scarcity: There is never enough of anything to satisfy all those who want it. The first lesson of politics is to disregard the first lesson of economics."

—Thomas Sowell

This is a very important book, not only for state and national legislators who try to represent citizens instead of special interests, but also for taxing and spending watchdogs in the press and those involved with good government citizen activist groups.

Like my own effort in the US Senate, then working with then Illinois Senator Barack Obama to pass fiscal transparency legislation into law, this book is non-partisan. It clearly refutes the now-popular myth that tax-cutting in Kansas caused a financial crisis there. It shows that *both* political parties in Kansas—specifically, their increased spending—were equally at fault for the crisis.

Almost all governments have a real knack for wasting money and doing things badly, and that's what happened to what, on paper, promised to be a marvelous tax relief effort in Kansas.

Those who wanted higher taxes said the Kansas tax cuts caused severe spending cuts. But what *really* happened was this: Kansas legislators *increased* spending as taxes were cut and then routinely set new spending records! The tax cutters received the blame for the financial crisis which followed, the spenders smiled all the way to reelection, and the special interests were *doubly* happy; their money was not only *not* cut off, it was increased!

At the same time, Democrats and Republicans alike largely ignored the recommendations of an independent efficiency study, among other commonsense suggestions, that would have reduced state government costs by about $2 billion over several years. For example: (1) using bulk purchasing to reduce costs and (2) putting a reasonable cap on school district cash reserves. Kansas school districts claimed to be underfunded while at the same time diverting money from classrooms into record-setting cash reserves.

Political decisions favoring special interests like the state's costly vendors' and school bureaucracies were, and are today, the primary cause of Kansas's budget issues.

There were also claims that tax cuts led to widespread tax avoidance schemes. This is simply false, as the authors demonstrate. While not all companies received tax cuts, those that did posted very strong job gains.

So what's behind the hue and cry over Kansas? Successful implementation of a major tax cut would have paved the way for growth and prosperity in Kansas, and since eliminating wasteful spending is the key to having lower taxes, those that profit from wasteful spending—the special interests and the legislators beholden to them—had strong incentives to demonize the tax-cutting plan and/or help its demise.

The Nobel Prize–winning economist James Buchanan explained why governments—particularly when they become too large and therefore very difficult to watch over and control—become wasteful when he developed what is now called "public choice economics." In just those few words what Buchanan demonstrated was that large bureaucracies, as well as legislators seeking re-election and then "golden" pensions when they retire, too often end up representing *what is good for them*, instead of for the taxpayers.

For example, on a lighter note for a minute—merely to give some absurd examples of how legislators and bureaucrats either keep themselves busy or pass out political favors—during my time in the House and Senate, I documented hundreds of ways federal tax dollars were wasted. Here are just a few from 2013:

The Popular Romance Project has received nearly $1 million from the National Endowment of the Humanities (NEH) since 2010 to "explore the fascinating, often contradictory origins and influences of popular romance as told in novels, films, comics, advice books, songs, and Internet fan fiction, taking a global perspective—while looking back across time as far as the ancient Greeks."

The National Institutes for Health spent $335,525 on a study that concluded wives would find marriage more satisfying if they could calm down faster during arguments with their husbands.

Fearing that rising temperatures could cause grass to grow more slowly, and in turn result in smaller cattle and bison that eat the grass, the US Department of Agriculture awarded a five-year, $9.6 million grant to Kansas State University to combat climate-induced bovine weight loss.

Who *benefits* from programs like these? Only the bureaucrats in large government agencies and their friends in the legislatures, not you the taxpayer.

Government and elected officials have a moral obligation to efficiently spend your money, and that's also the key to having lower taxes.

The plain-speaking economist Frederic Bastiat once wrote, "The worst thing that can happen to a good cause is, not to be skillfully attacked, but to be poorly defended." This book will show legislators and citizen activists everywhere how *effectively* to defend tax and spending reforms against those who use "The Kansas Myth" to attack their efforts.

Soon, I hope, we Americans will be able to keep more of our hard-earned income while forcing governments to operate more efficiently and effectively. The place to start is with *What was* Really *the Matter with the Kansas Tax Plan*.

Senator Coburn is the author of Breach of Trust, The Debt Bomb, *and* Smashing the DC Monopoly.

Introduction

"A lie gets halfway around the world before the truth has a chance to get its pants on."

—Sir Winston Churchill

For all that's been written about tax reform passed by the 2012 Kansas legislature, much of its history has either not been recorded or has been skewed to fit political agendas favoring higher taxes and more government spending. The Kansas tax-relief effort was officially killed when the 2017 Kansas legislature overrode Governor Brownback's veto and imposed the largest tax increase in Kansas's history—but distortions of the real story continue in order to discourage other states from reducing taxes and were even used to undermine federal tax reform efforts in late 2017.

The purpose of this book is not to determine whether tax relief in Kansas "worked." Indeed, given that the original plan was never fully implemented, that taxes were increased in 2013 and 2015, and the effort occurred during the implementation of Obamacare and downturns in two important Kansas economic sectors (agriculture, oil and gas), any attempt to do so would likely be so full of caveats as to be rendered meaningless. Rather, the purpose is to help citizens and elected officials across the nation (and maybe even future Kansas legislators) learn from the mistakes made in Kansas in their efforts to reduce taxes down the road and create the best path forward for everyone to achieve prosperity.

Some of the false information was probably spread innocently by people repeating what they were told, but that's no excuse for the media. Even editorials should be based on verified facts, but instead, hearsay that fit a pre-determined narrative quite often sufficed.

The *Washington Post*, for example, opined, "Mr. Brownback's Kansas trial is rapidly becoming a cautionary tale for conservative governors elsewhere who have blithely peddled the theology of tax cuts as a painless panacea for sluggish growth."[1]

The *Post* editorial dated September 21, 2014, said Kansas had cut per-pupil school funding by more than 10 percent between 2008 and 2014, but that simply wasn't true. Information of that nature was routinely bandied about by tax-relief opponents, but the *Post* apparently didn't bother to check the facts. According to the Kansas Department of Education, both State Aid and Total Funding were higher in 2014 than in 2008.[2]

Table 1: Per-Pupil Funding		
School Year	State	Total
2005	$ 5,346	$ 9,707
2006	$ 6,006	$ 10,596
2007	$ 6,494	$ 11,558
2008	$ 7,008	$ 12,188
2009	$ 7,344	$ 12,660
2010	$ 6,326	$ 12,330
2011	$ 6,511	$ 12,283
2012	$ 6,983	$ 12,656
2013	$ 6,984	$ 12,781
2014	$ 7,088	$ 12,960
Source: Kansas Dept. of Education		

Media routinely talked about state spending reductions, including this 2016 comment from the *New York Times*: "Sweeping cutbacks ranged from basic welfare to the state university system."[3] One would never know from statements of this nature that spending actually increased over the years.

General Fund spending increased in Fiscal Year 2013 and set a new record at $6.135 billion. Another spending record was set in FY 2015 at $6.237 billion and Kansas finished FY 2017 with yet another record at $6.302 billion.[4] The annual rate of spending growth was less than prior years and agencies didn't receive as much money as most wanted, so that's a "cut" in government parlance—but not in reality.

Kansas has also been made the poster-child for resisting federal tax reform. A *Politico* op-ed from May 4, 2017, by Tax Foundation employees Kyle Pomerleau, Scott Drenkard, and John Buhl, is a good example of the attempts to dissuade tax-relief efforts with partial storytelling and a false claim thrown in for good measure.[5] "The one-page tax plan that President Donald Trump's administration released last week didn't offer much detail. But its proposal to lower taxes for certain types of smaller businesses stood out—because the idea has been tried before at the state level and backfired." The authors attribute Kansas's budget issues to exempting pass-through income of entities not organized as C-corporations from state income tax, contending that the exemption for LLCs, sub-S corporations, partnerships, and proprietors encouraged a massive tax-avoidance scheme.

They said, "When the exemption was passed in 2012, Kansas officials estimated that 191,000 entities would newly take advantage of it. But the exemption created a massive tax-avoidance scheme: Many savvy taxpayers, both individuals and corporations, ended up restructuring as pass-through entities so they wouldn't have to pay taxes. The latest figures from the state show that there are 330,000 pass-through exemption claimants as of 2015—almost double what was originally anticipated."

Claims of that nature were routinely made by media and other opponents of tax relief in general and the pass-through exemption in particular, but it was all conjecture. As you'll learn later in the book, the Department of Revenue's estimate of the number of filers was just an unfortunate mistake that wasn't corrected until Kansas Policy Institute found IRS data in May 2017 showing that the original estimate *should* have been around 330,000 based on existing tax filers.[6] Other research also refutes notions of massive tax avoidance; there was a little, but that wasn't the cause of state budget issues.

The Tax Foundation eventually published corrections of its tax-avoidance claim and other errors on its website, but the damage done in the previous months and years could have been avoided had they—and many others, including media—done some research.

Media and others have also claimed that Governor Brownback and conservative legislators believed the tax cuts would pay for themselves; they claimed that Kansans wanted a giant personal income tax hike on low- and middle-income families, and that Governor Brownback went back on his word to the senate in order to pass the original legislation. Distortions like these and others described throughout the book were unfortunately quite common and seemed devised as scare tactics to go along with the "Don't be like Kansas" message delivered to elected officials around the country. If large-scale tax relief could be pulled off in Kansas, it would encourage a wave of similar action in other states, and those who prefer higher taxes and more government spending couldn't allow that to happen—so Kansas's efforts had to be demonized.

Downplaying or ignoring success in other areas was another symptom of what would be diagnosed as "Brownback Derangement Syndrome" (BDS) among media. Here are just a few of those successes from the limited government/personal freedom perspective.

- There has been continued resistance to Medicaid expansion under Obamacare, which, according to an analysis by Dr. Jagadeesh Gokhale (then a Cato Institute scholar and sitting member of the Social Security Advisory Board), would have imposed a ten-year cost of $13 billion on taxpayers including the interest and debt service on federal borrowing for expansion.[7]
- The state's Medicaid program switched to a privatized managed-care system, saving roughly $1 billion over five years.[8]
- Stronger work requirements put in place for welfare

recipients paid big dividends for both welfare recipients and the state of Kansas. According to the Foundation for Government Accountability, "Kansas families who left welfare under the new sanctions saw their earnings more than double, increasing by an average of 104 percent within just one year." FGA also noted that higher income more than offset the loss of Temporary Assistance to Needy Families (TANF) and able-bodied adult enrollment in TANF dropped 78 percent from 2011 to 2017.[9]

- A tax-credit scholarship program for low-income students attending the state's ninety-nine worst-performing schools was approved in 2014. It remains the only school choice option available in Kansas.[10]
- A new cash balance pension system was created for new state and school employees hired after January 1, 2015.[11] Cash balance plans are often called "hybrids" because they operate similarly to a 401k plan with employees making pre-tax contributions, but there is a guaranteed minimal annual interest earning (4 percent in the Kansas plan).
- Multiple property tax reforms were passed, making the appeals process more taxpayer-friendly, and a voter empowerment law requires an affirmative public vote if cities and counties wish to increase certain property tax revenue beyond the rate of inflation.

Kansas's hoped-for economic growth didn't all materialize (partly because the plan passed in 2012 was never fully implemented and other reasons explained throughout the book), but there were some gains in private sector employment. It's true that Kansas continues to trail national averages, but media accounts rarely, if ever, reported that historically trailing national averages was about as common as the wind blowing in Kansas.

Bureau of Economic Analysis (BEA) data shows Kansas was ranked #40 among the states for private sector job growth between 1998 and 2012.[12] Over the first four years since tax relief, however, Kansas was ranked #37 in private-sector job growth.[13] (We use BEA data to capture full employment because the Bureau of Labor Statistics [BLS] does not include farm workers or proprietors.)

Table 2: Employment by Legal Entity Type					
State of Kansas					
Entity Type	Employees on March 12			Percent Change	
	2010	2012	2015	2010-12	2012-15
Corporations	535,839	530,567	535,109	-1.0%	0.9%
Pass-Through	418,544	428,593	483,017	2.4%	12.7%
Non-profits	143,726	143,815	141,864	0.1%	-1.4%
Other	10,834	11,788	10,513	8.8%	-10.8%
Private	1,108,943	1,114,763	1,170,503	0.5%	5.0%
United States (000)					
Entity Type	Employees (000) on March 12			Percent Change	
	2010	2012	2015	2010-12	2012-15
Corporations	51,829	53,510	54,849	3.2%	2.5%
Pass-Through	43,387	45,374	51,661	4.6%	13.9%
Non-profits	15,020	15,238	15,744	1.5%	3.3%
Other	532	530	541	-0.5%	2.2%
Private	110,768	114,652	122,795	3.5%	7.1%
Source: U.S. Census, Employment by Legal Form of Organization					

Private sector job growth for pass-through employers shows stronger gains than C-corporation employment. The US Census tracks employment by Legal Form or Organization and began publishing state-level data in 2010.[14] Over the two years preceding the exemption on pass-through income, jobs at pass-through entities tracked by the BLS grew by just 2.4 percent compared to the national average of 4.6 percent, or 52 percent of the national average. Over the three years following implementation of the pass-through exemption, employment at pass-through entities grew at 92 percent of the national average (12.7 percent vs. 13.9 percent). The raw data shows the 54,424 jobs added by pass-through employers accounted for 98 percent of all private-sector job growth in Kansas.

However, the actual impact of the exemption on pass-through job creation is less than the raw data would indicate, as some of those jobs added as pass-through employers came from C-corporations that converted. "Kansas Tax Policy and Economy Review" published by the Kansas Department of Revenue (KDOR) reports a decline of 10,325 W-2s associated with C-corporation conversion in 2013 and 2014; but even if every W-2 represented a job conversion, some of that would be offset by the gain in new proprietors not included in the Census data. Census gets its data from the BLS, which doesn't track proprietors that have no employees, and the BEA shows Kansas added 23,981 proprietors between 2012 and 2015; some of those new proprietors could represent jobs not captured in BLS data.[15]

Chart 1
Kansas vs Missouri Income Tax Migration
Adjusted Aggregate Gross Income, Adjusted to 2015 Dollars
In Millions

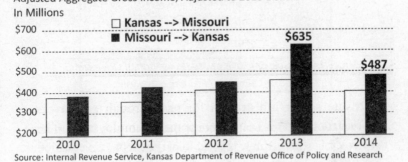

Source: Internal Revenue Service, Kansas Department of Revenue Office of Policy and Research

Then again, not all of the C-corporation employment declines and pass-through gains can be attributed to corporate conversions. IRS migration data shows a 41 percent spike in Adjusted Gross Income moving from Missouri to Kansas in 2013, followed by another strong gain of nearly a half-billion dollars in 2014. And the extent to which pass-through jobs were disproportionately impacted by declines in agriculture and the oil and gas sectors is also unknown.

Governor Brownback's goal of "beating Missouri" with lower taxes, though, was gaining ground. Kansas continued to outperform the Missouri side of the fourteen-county Kansas City Metropolitan Statistical Area (MSA)[16] following the tax cuts that went into effect in 2013.

Table 3: Private Nonfarm Jobs Kansas City Metro			
County	2012	2015	% Chg.
Johnson, KS	386,089	418,378	8.4%
Leavenworth, KS	19,173	19,792	3.2%
Linn, KS	2,365	2,563	8.4%
Miami, KS	9,678	10,099	4.4%
Wyandotte, KS	83,814	90,254	7.7%
Kansas total	501,119	541,086	8.0%
Bates, MO	4,285	4,774	11.4%
Caldwell, MO	1,946	2,157	10.8%
Cass, MO	29,564	31,914	7.9%
Clay, MO	102,575	114,515	11.6%
Clinton, MO	5,315	5,473	3.0%
Jackson, MO	384,735	402,470	4.6%
Lafayette, MO	10,821	10,576	-2.3%
Platte, MO	49,448	52,293	5.8%
Ray, MO	4,707	5,052	7.3%
Missouri total	593,396	629,224	6.0%
Source: Bureau of Economic Analysis			

Private nonfarm employment data from the BEA in the above table shows the Kansas side of the MSA grew by 8 percent in the first three years compared to 6 percent growth on the Missouri side. The gap is even wider in the two largest counties, with Johnson County, Kansas, growing by 8.4 percent and neighboring Jackson County, Missouri, only having 4.6 percent job growth. Kansas also experienced an increase in the compound annual growth rate (CAGR) after taxes were reduced. The MSA annual rate improved from

1.06 percent over the ten years leading up to tax relief to 1.92 percent in the next three years; Johnson County went from 1.19 percent annual growth to 2.03 percent annual growth.[17]

BEA data is used for these job comparisons because it's more comprehensive than that provided by the Bureau of Labor Statistics. BLS oddly does not include farm workers or proprietors with no employees in its data, whereas BEA includes everything. The downside of BEA employment data is that it is only published on an annual basis; at the time this was written, 2016 state-level data had been published, but county-level data was only published through 2015.

The true extent to which the tax plan affected job growth cannot be ascertained for many reasons, including but not limited to it being reversed only five years after initial passage, minor amounts of organizational restructuring, economic downturns in aviation, agriculture and the oil and gas sectors, and the constant pressure to reverse the tax cuts. The degree to which some gains and losses would have occurred regardless of tax policy is also unknown. But it can be said with certainty that the tax plan did not crater the Kansas economy as has been alleged, and as explained later, Kansas did see a noticeable increase in the number of new business filings.

To be sure, mistakes were made in the implementation of tax relief in Kansas; most notably, spending was increased after taxes were cut, and taxes were increased in 2013 and 2015 after Democrats and many Republicans refused to reduce the cost of government. (By the way, with the exception of former Senate President Steve Morris, all interview invitations for this book sent to Democrats and Republicans who wouldn't propose spending reductions or tax increases leading up to the 2016 election were ignored or declined.) And it is a gross understatement to say that the messaging on the rationale and need for implementing a tax cut left a lot to be desired.

Mistakes of all flavors are documented throughout the book and summarized in Chapter 7 so that future tax-relief proponents are better prepared. But scare tactics and Kansas's mistakes shouldn't be deterrents to much-needed tax relief across the nation.

Recounting everything that occurred between inspiration and the final destruction of the Kansas tax-relief effort would produce a five-pound tome, so the wisdom of Antoine de Saint-Exupéry guided the writing and editing process: "Perfection is achieved, not when there is nothing more to add, but when there is nothing left to take away."

We hope you believe we accomplished our mission.

1

Motivations for Tax Relief

"You got to be careful if you don't know where you're going, because you might not get there."

—Yogi Berra

Four former Kansas governors—John Carlin, Mike Hayden, Bill Graves, and Kathleen Sebelius—announced the formation of a political organization on June 24, 2016, to raise money for candidates who opposed tax relief and would return Kansas to "fiscal health."[18] And true to form, media dutifully made many in-kind contributions to their 501(c)(4) with a flurry of articles and editorials touting the good old days under the previous governors' reigns and scolding Governor Brownback and anyone else who wanted to let Kansans keep more of their hard-earned money. Had media bothered to look, they would have found that "fiscal health" during the reign of those former governors was more akin to a slowly sinking ship.[19]

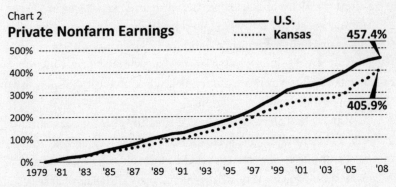

Chart 2
Private Nonfarm Earnings

——— U.S.
········· Kansas

457.4%

405.9%

Source: Bureau of Economic Analysis

Private Nonfarm Earnings, a major component of Personal Income, was growing a little faster than the national average in 1980 and 1981 but then began falling further and further behind throughout those governors' reigns. Nominal Private Nonfarm Earnings grew by 457.4 percent between 1979 and 2008, but the growth in Kansas was just 405.9 percent.[20]

Chart 3

Private Nonfarm Jobs

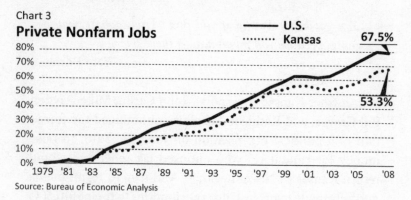

Source: Bureau of Economic Analysis

Kansas was falling even farther behind in private job growth and the gap became noticeably worse in the last eight years of their reign. Kansas experienced Private Nonfarm Job growth of 53.3 percent between 1979 and 2008, or about 79 percent of the national average, which grew by 67.5 percent.[21]

Those former governors, media, and their friends excoriated the Brownback administration and the legislature for not having structurally balanced budgets (tax revenue meeting or exceeding spending), and for having a school funding lawsuit, credit downgrades, and a threatened school closure by the Kansas Supreme Court. But while that did happen, it was like déjà vu all over again.

Kansas had already had multiple school funding lawsuits and a threatened school closure under the former vaunted governments. The state's credit outlook was also downgraded before Governor Brownback took office, and at least in one case, for eerily similar reasons.[22] In an August 2002 report about Kansas being placed on a credit watch list, the *Topeka Capital-Journal* said, "Legislators ended the 2002 session with a budget reserve of nearly 5 percent. However, continued declines in revenue collections took that balance down to less than 1 percent on July 31, the end of fiscal year 2002. 'That makes us financially vulnerable,' [then State Budget Director Duane] Goossen said, adding that the state continues to borrow from other internal funds to meet daily demands for revenue. James Breeding, a credit analyst with Standard & Poor's, said the road to financial health could prove challenging because the state has relied on one-time measures to fund part of the recent shortfalls. He noted the reduction in the state's cash reserves to help cover the gap in the state's $4.4 billion budget."[23]

Goossen often chimed in with the former governors to criticize Kansas, including this comment on the importance of having structurally balanced budgets: "The Kansas budget has been structurally unbalanced every year since the 2012/2013 tax cuts went into effect, putting the state in a highly precarious financial situation."[24] Listening to media and others opposed to tax relief, one would think that spending exceeding revenue was a phenomenon created by the 2012 tax relief, but that was another of those long-standing Kansas traditions. Over the sixteen-year span from 1993 to 2008, General Fund spending exceeded General Fund tax revenue eight times.[25]

Escalating Pension and Medicaid Costs

In addition to substandard economic growth, there was also a significant self-inflicted pension funding crisis. The legislature increased pension benefits by 25 percent effective July 1, 1993, by increasing the participating service rate multiplier from 1.40 percent to 1.75 percent.[26] Simultaneously, the legislature also made the unbelievable decision to restrict employer contributions to fund pension benefits for school employees and state and local government employees. Instead of making the Annually Required Contribution (ARC), legislation passed in 1993 stipulated that employer contribution rates could not increase by more than a statutory cap.[27]

For example, the December 31, 2009, Kansas Public Employees Retirement System (KPERS) Valuation Report listed the ARC rate for school employees at 14.69 percent of payroll, but the statutory rate was only 9.37 percent of payroll, thereby shorting the employer contribution by 5.32 percent of payroll that year. The employer contribution was shorted by 2.1 percent of payroll for local government employees and by 0.18 percent for state employees.[28]

By 2011, higher benefits, insufficient employer contributions, and a deep recession prompted Morningstar to list Kansas among the twenty-one states whose state pension systems were not fiscally sound.[29] Morningstar put Kansas's funding ratio at just 59.2 percent and tied for the forty-second worst-funded ratio among the fifty states. Funding ratios, however, are predicated upon the assumed rate of return on investments, which was 8 percent for Kansas. A 2016 report from the American Legislative Exchange Council (ALEC) recently ranked state pension plans using a more realistic funding ratio, which shows the Kansas pension system funded at just 29.9 percent.[30]

The ALEC report "uses a rate of return based on the equivalent of a hypothetical 15-year US Treasury bond yield. Since this is not presently offered as an investment instrument, the number is derived from an average of the 10- and 20-year bond yields. This year's number is averaged from March 2015 to March 2016. The resulting rate is 2.344 percent, which is considered a 'risk-free' rate."[31]

The report also quotes former Social Security Administration Deputy Commissioner Andrew Biggs and economist Kent Smetters, who have explained, "No matter how well a pension plan manages its investments, it cannot generate 8 percent returns with certainty." The greater the gap between a risk-free investment assumption and assumed rate, the more state budgets—and ultimately citizens—are exposed to additional risk and funding shortfalls.

Chart 4
Pension Funding % of General Fund Spending

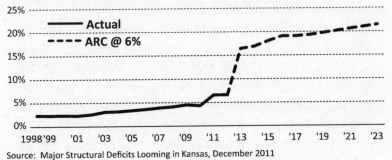

Source: Major Structural Deficits Looming in Kansas, December 2011

Chart 5
Pension & Medicaid % of General Fund Spending

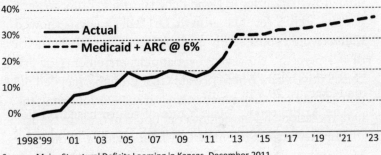

Source: Major Structural Deficits Looming in Kansas, December 2011

A 2011 study by Dr. Art Hall, executive director of the Center for Applied Economics at the University of Kansas School of Business, put that risk into perspective by estimating the impact of funding the Annually Required Contribution for KPERS at an assumed investment return rate of 6 percent instead of 8 percent, using funding projections provided by the KPERS actuaries.[32] KPERS pension funding had already grown from 2.3 percent of General Fund spending to 6.6 percent between 1998 and 2011. Assuming General Fund spending would expand as required for the higher pension funding, Medicaid would continue to grow without Obamacare, and all other spending would increase at the historic average rate, Dr. Hall found that KPERS pension funding would consume 21.5 percent of General Fund spending by FY 2023.

Kansas was also having to deal with runaway Medicaid costs, which had gone from 3.5 percent of General Fund spending in 1998 to 13.2 percent in 2011. Collectively, KPERS pension funding at a 6 percent assumed investment return and existing Medicaid (without Obamacare) were projected to consume 37 percent of General Fund spending by FY 2023.

But that wasn't all of the bad news. In order for all other spending to increase at the historic average along with funding higher pension costs and the growth in Medicaid, revenue would have to consistently exceed 5 percent annual growth in order to avoid deficits. And in order to get 5 percent annual revenue growth, Dr. Hall's analysis showed Kansas would consistently need private sector GDP growth of 6.5 percent. However, overlapping increments of five consecutive years where private GDP growth exceeded 6.5 percent had only happened in the early 1980s following the 1982 recession and in the dot-com boom of the late 1990s.

This scenario presented legislators with a choice: let Medicaid and pension funding dramatically crowd out spending on everything else, significantly increase the already high tax burden, or take steps to increase economic growth to get more revenue.

Those wanting to return to the policies of the former governors may have thought they were going back to "fiscal health," but to put it in a Yogiism, they didn't know where they were going and they weren't going to get there.

Desire to Reverse Economic Stagnation

Asked what prompted the decision to cut taxes, those inti-mately involved with developing plans to do so responded with several variations on a similar theme. Former Chair of the House Taxation Committee Richard Carlson and Senator Ty Masterson expressed a desire to move Kansas away from being a high-tax state relative to other states in the region in order to stimulate job growth.

Carlson said, "Every state surrounding Kansas had a lower income tax rate with the exception of Nebraska . . . and if you go to Travis Brown's website [HowMoneyWalks.com], Kansas had in-migration of [Adjusted Gross Income] only from one surrounding state and that was Nebraska. It wasn't a lot but at least we had a little bit from that state." Carlson also cited a lag in GDP growth relative to Plains states.

Once Kansas cut taxes, however, Missouri joined Nebraska in being an exporter of AGI to Kansas. IRS mi-gration data shows Kansas had a net gain of $235.4 million in Adjusted Gross Income moving from Missouri to Kansas in the first three years that tax cuts were in effect,[33] and that put Kansas into a long-term net gain position.

HowMoneyWalks.com shows that the $235.4 million gain following the tax cuts put Kansas into a long-term net gain of $131.65 million in Adjusted Gross Income from Missouri between 1992 and 2015 (the most recent data available as this book was written). Kansas's five largest AGI

Table 4: Kansas Adjusted Gross Income Gains and Losses between 1992 and 2015	
Top Five Gains:	
California	$176.43 million
Missouri	$131.65 million
Nebraska	$104.34 million
Iowa	$99.02 million
Illinois	$85.97 million
Top Five Losses:	
Texas	$1.46 billion
Florida	$971.72 million
Colorado	$578.07 million
Oklahoma	$432.61 million
Arizona	$403.56 million
Source: HowMoneyWalks.com; accessed July 26, 2017	

gains over that period came from California residents ($176.4 million), followed by Missouri, Nebraska ($104.3 million), Iowa ($99.2 million), and Illinois ($86 million). Kansas's greatest AGI loss was to Texas ($1.46 billion), followed by Florida ($971.7 million). Colorado ($578.1 million) and Oklahoma are the third and fourth largest net AGI outflow states, respectively.

Former Secretary of Revenue Nick Jordan said Governor Brownback pushed tax cuts from day one on the transition team (preparing to take office): "We're going to lower taxes and we're going to create jobs." Jordan says the governor instructed his team to figure out the best way to do it.

Governor Brownback's motivation was a combination of Kansas-specific issues as well as a national historical perspective: "I've been studying this for a long period of time. I'm a friend of Art Laffer and I've worked with Art for a long period of time. I believed in the Reagan tax cuts. I saw them. I saw their impact on the economy. I had been working with [Art Laffer] after I made these kinds of proposals when I was in the Congress, going to a flat-tax system nationwide. Paul Ryan was on my staff, who's committed to supply side, I am, too. That's what we need. And then, I kept looking at the migration data, and it was just exactly what you thought it would be for Kansas. We were getting people from higher-tax states to Kansas, and we were losing them to lower-tax states.

"And we've gotta stop losing so many Kansans, because we [are] just continuing to drift down on our [share of population relative to the other 49 states]. . . . We're just continuing to slowly decline. The only way we can stop that is to get a more economic vibrant environment. And the only way we can do that is to get our income taxes down with the objective of getting [to] zero income tax. I've been committed to that path for a long period of time and spent a lot of time really trying to study it, looking at it, looking at what other countries have done on flat taxes."

Persistent negative domestic migration doesn't just impact the local economy and the state budget, Governor Brownback noted. "[Senator Bob] Dole was first elected to the sixth congressional district in Kansas. We're down to four, headed to three. I've seen it in Iowa, losing congressional power."

Governor Brownback also recalled a physical manifestation of tax policy when he was running for president in 2008. "You could physically see it. And the one I remember the most was Sioux City, Iowa, and Sioux Falls, South Dakota . . . If you didn't know where you were, you'd say the topography of those areas looks the same. And everybody campaigns a lot in Iowa. When I'm running for president, I'm campaigning up there. And then, I'd been in Sioux Falls previously, but you'd go across the line, everything's newer in Sioux Falls than it is in Sioux City.

"You go to Sioux City, and it looks older. All the recent money has gone to Sioux Falls, well, why? Well, they have no income tax in Sioux Falls. And you can see it in New Hampshire and New England states. You go up there and you look at the data; this just jumps at you."

Getting the Incentives Right

The governor also spoke of the long-standing border war for jobs between Kansas and Missouri, which had historically been driven by tax subsidies given to individual businesses to incent them to cross state lines. "Our biggest play had to be to win the battle for Kansas City. Our best long-term near-term economic play is to win the battle for Kansas City. Why do that? Get your income taxes down. That's the clearest thing I can do. And I said often in the campaign running for governor, so we don't have to beat the world, but we do have to beat Missouri."

Kansas had been staying ahead of Missouri in the Kansas City Metropolitan Area in private sector job growth using tax incentives; however, the tax subsidies given to companies such as AMC Theatres and Applebee's were largely a waste of taxpayer money. One such program, Promoting Employment Across Kansas (PEAK) was the subject of a study conducted by then Washington University (St. Louis) professor Nathan Jenson, which contains this stark statement:

> The paper's main finding is that, when comparing firms receiving PEAK incentives to a similar set of "control" firms, PEAK incentives recipients are statistically not more likely to generate new jobs than similar firms not receiving incentives. A secondary set of findings shows that firms relocating to Kansas, with or without incentives, do not experience job growth at higher rates than existing firms.[34]

While tax subsidies continue to be used by Missouri and Kansas, both states have signaled interest in a subsidy cease fire. The *Kansas City Star* reported that Missouri passed 2014 legislation "to curtail the area's economic border war," but Kansas didn't agree to the plan.[35] Governor Brownback said Kansas would halt some of its business tax incentives, but his offer would have required Missouri to take legislative action. The *Star* said under Brownback's proposal that "both states would be required to refrain from actively recruiting in each other's border counties. But, Brownback said, the states also should develop a process to offer incentives when there's a legitimate threat of a company leaving the metro area."

Nothing had developed from Brownback's proposal as this book was written, but data provided in the *KC Star* article underscores the absurdity of tax subsidy programs. "Since 2009, 5,702 jobs have moved from Jackson County [Missouri] to Johnson or Wyandotte counties [Kansas] using PEAK incentives, and 3,998 jobs have moved from

Johnson or Wyandotte counties to Jackson County with Missouri Works incentives." Bill Hall, assistant to the chairman of Hallmark Cards, said incentive-based moves had cost $262 million in lost tax revenues, for a subsidy cost of about $60,000 per job involved.[36]

Dr. Art Hall was consulted frequently on the tax structure and state economic conditions by Secretary Jordan, Representative Carlson, Senator Masterson, and other legislative leaders. Hall is credited with designing the expensing provision contained in House Substitute for SB 196 that passed in the 2011 legislative session. According to the bill's Supplemental Note, taxpayers can claim a full expense deduction (rather than depreciation) for the cost of certain machinery and equipment depreciable under Section 138 of the Internal Revenue Service code and certain canned software placed into service beginning in tax year 2012. Any property sold during the applicable recovery period defined by federal law or relocated outside the state during such period would be subject to having a portion of its expense deduction recaptured for Kansas income tax purposes. Taxpayers electing to expense qualified investments are prohibited from also claiming a number of existing tax subsidies, which was not only good policy but also a smart way to offset the revenue loss associated with immediate expensing.[37]

Dr. Hall's efforts also led to a 2006 tax change that exempts new business machinery and equipment from the personal property tax.

Solving the Productivity Puzzle

Hall also worked with the Brownback transition team and said there was agreement on the desire to cut taxes and that Governor Brownback was particularly focused on doing something to reverse population loss from persistent net domestic out–migration. Hall's motivation for reducing taxes was centered on what he called "solving the productivity puzzle," with productivity defined as inflation-adjusted GDP divided by the total number of full- and part-time workers in the economy—a dollar value of output per worker.

Hall said, "[The Brandmeyer Center for Applied Economics] had a scholar, Peter Orazem, visiting from Iowa State, and he did this productivity thing and we couldn't identify a reason for it at the time, so we just called it a puzzle."

A white paper by Dr. Hall that was adapted from testimony provided to the house and senate taxation committees in January 2006 dives deeply into the issue (Hall's testimony also prompted the initial attempt to pass his "expensing" concept that finally was adopted in 2011). From *Local Government and the Kansas Productivity Puzzle:*

> The Kansas economy suffers from an odd anomaly that has direct consequences for the economic well-being of Kansans. For reasons that have no ready explanation, the Kansas economy lags both the nation and the region in terms of per-worker productivity and the growth rate of per-worker productivity. This anomaly began about 20 years ago, and has had direct implications for the growth of per-worker compensation.
>
> Chart 1 illustrates a set of trend lines that embody important information about the implications of the "Kansas Productivity Puzzle." It depicts relative, inflation-adjusted growth rates—among the U.S., the Plains region, and Kansas—of a metric called Gross State Product (GSP). Like Gross Domestic Product (GDP) at the national level, GSP measures the total dollar value of all goods and services produced within a state's borders during a given year. Over the twenty-seven-year period shown (the years of best data availability), the collection of all U.S. states' GSP combined has grown 130 percent, the collection of Plains

states combined has grown 99 percent, and Kansas GSP has grown 92 percent. (The Plains states include Iowa, Kansas, Minnesota, Missouri, Nebraska, North Dakota, and South Dakota.)

Chart 1:
Trends in Economic Growth (GSP)
Kansas Lags the U.S. and the Plains States

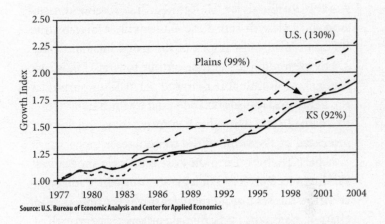

Source: U.S. Bureau of Economic Analysis and Center for Applied Economics

Productivity differences account for about half of the economic growth difference between Kansas and the U.S. (The other half relates to Kansas' slower employment growth.) Productivity differences account for virtually 100 percent of the growth difference between Kansas and the Plains region.

Economic growth for an economy works just like compound interest for an investment: Small differences in rates make a big difference over time. On an average annual basis, the GSP growth rates illustrated in Chart 1 equal 3.1 percent for the U.S., 2.5 percent for the Plains, and 2.4 percent for Kansas. If Kansas GSP had grown at the U.S. average annual rate of 3.1 percent instead of 2.4 percent (a difference of 0.7 percentage points), the Kansas economy would have been about

$18 billion dollars richer in 2004—or about $10,000 per worker. If Kansas GSP had grown at the Plains average annual rate of 2.5 percent, the Kansas economy would have been about $2 billion dollars richer in 2004—or about $1,300 per worker.

Productivity is defined as (inflation-adjusted) GSP divided by the total number of full and part-time workers in the economy—a dollar value of output per worker. Productivity, so defined, has a value dimension and a growth-rate dimension, as illustrated by the different levels and slopes of the trend lines in Chart 2. For example, per-worker output for the U.S. is, on average, more valuable than the per-worker output in the Plains and Kansas (as indicated by the height of the trend lines), and that value has grown more quickly (as indicated by the slope of the trend lines).

Chart 2 helps inform the core aspects of the Kansas Productivity Puzzle. At first glance, one can readily perceive the Kansas productivity lag. Over the time period charted, Kansas has experienced productivity growth of 26 percent; the U.S. and Plains region have experienced productivity growth of 38 percent and 30 percent, respectively. Total productivity growth in Kansas ranks 37th among the states. The key feature of the puzzle, however, is the fact that the lag shown in Chart 2 persists across all industry sectors, with exceptions during certain time periods for durable goods manufacturing and transportation and public utilities. The observer is tempted to focus on the 1995 productivity dip in Kansas, but the lag relative to the Plains begins about 1986. (Small differences over time make a big difference.)

Chart 2:
Trends in Labor Productivity
Kansas Lags the U.S. and the Plains States

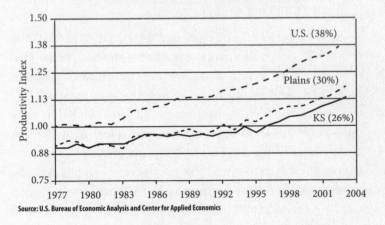

Source: U.S. Bureau of Economic Analysis and Center for Applied Economics

Kansas' lagging productivity matters because productivity drives both business competitiveness and
worker compensation. Over the past quarter century,
as economic theory predicts, there is a near perfect
statistical correlation in Kansas between productivity growth and per-worker compensation (wages plus
employer-paid benefits and taxes). Because Kansas
lags in productivity, it also lags in terms of per-worker
compensation. In fact, a chart illustrating trends in per-
worker compensation would look almost identical to
the trend lines on Chart 2.[38]

Dr. Hall now attributes the productivity lag that began
in 1986 to a property tax issue, saying, "It's hard to prove
but I believe it's because of the 1986 state constitutional
amendment dealing with property tax. The basic story was
that for two or three decades there was a big debate over
property tax values being way off." Taxpayer frustration finally prompted the legislature to propose a constitutional

amendment, which established a substantial new property classification system and revaluation that voters approved in November 1986. The application of the new classification system and the results of reappraisal took place in January 1989.

In *A History of Tax Policy in Kansas,* Dr. Hall explains that while revaluation was overall revenue neutral to government, there were devastating shifts in tax burden among individuals and businesses. "Widespread reappraisals had the practical effect of shifting tax burdens. And shift they did—once the state implemented the reforms in 1989. A comparison of the 1985 and 1990 property tax burdens on hypothetical (but identical) properties revealed homesteads experienced property tax increases of 357 percent; commercial properties experienced increases of 298 percent; and industrial properties experienced increases of 44 percent. Furthermore, the post-reform tax burden increases tended to persist."[39]

It was clear from speaking to Governor Brownback's team and key legislators over the years that they were aware of the economic challenges facing Kansas. The governor emphasized that tax cuts were intended to spur the economy; in his 2012 State of the State Address he said, "The economy remains one of our most pressing issues. While there are certainly factors a state cannot control when it comes to its economy, taxes are one area we do control. And when it comes to taxes, we have some of the highest in the region. This hurts our economic growth and job creation."[40]

No Messaging Strategy
But while some key players may have understood there were reasons for tax relief beyond wanting to let people keep more of their hard-earned money, the public and even many legislators were largely uninformed . . . and that would prove to be a fatal flaw. Kansans were told that cutting taxes would

make things better, but they didn't know the cold hard facts of anemic job growth, persistent net domestic out-migration and looming budget shortfalls from Medicaid and pension funding. Pushing a solution instead of first gaining citizens' understanding that a serious problem exists is an all-too-common mistake in the public policy arena. The political temptation to emphasize the upside, avoid discussion of past actions that created serious problems, and the resultant need for change outside one's comfort zone all often contribute to the undoing of good ideas, and that was certainly the case with the Kansas tax-relief effort.

In addition to a lack of clarity on the important reasons to consider tax relief, there was an abundance of legislative inertia. Explaining why it can be so frustrating to move issues through the legislature, Richard Carlson once said, "You have to understand . . . many legislators love progress, but they don't care much for change."

Economist Thomas Sowell is more blunt: "No one will really understand politics until they understand that politicians are not trying to solve our problems. They are trying to solve their own problems—of which getting elected and re-elected are No. 1 and No. 2. Whatever is No. 3 is far behind."

Some politicians are truly trying to solve problems, but they're in the minority. And absent pressure from concerned voters and/or a deep understanding of the potential stark consequences of *not* (in this case) cutting taxes to improve the state's economic trajectory, it would become much easier for many legislators in both parties to resist the needed spending adjustments and focus on priorities No. 1 and No. 2.

2

Designing Governor Brownback's
Tax Plan

"The significant problems we face cannot be solved at the same level of thinking we were at when we created them."
—Albert Einstein

The tax-relief legislation signed into law in 2012—Senate Substitute for House Bill 2117 (hereinafter HB 2117)—was not the bill proposed by Governor Brownback; that soap opera is chronicled in Chapter 3. The governor's 2012 proposal was also not the original tax-relief effort for individuals. That honor went to House Substitute for Senate Bill 1 (H Sub SB 1), introduced in the 2011 legislative session and dubbed the March to Economic Growth Act (MEGA).[41] According to Kansas Legislative Research Department (KLRD), "The original [SB 1] dealt with sales tax rate disclosures for retailers. The house Taxation Committee on March 15 [2011] voted to strip the bill's original provisions, insert the provisions of HB 2381, and recommend that a substitute bill be created."[42]

Bill substitution is a Kansas-specific process whereby legislation that has passed one chamber can be stripped of its contents and new subject material substituted; and once passed by the substituting chamber, it is sent back to the original chamber for consideration. MEGA passed the house by a vote 73–47 with five legislators not voting. It was then sent to the senate, which ruled that the original SB 1 had been materially changed and referred it to the senate

Assessment and Taxation Committee, where the bill eventually died in committee.

House Taxation Chairman Richard Carlson and Senator Ty Masterson were the primary architects of H Sub SB 1. The concept was to use the percentage change in revenue for a specific set of General Fund tax receipts (primarily income, privilege, and excise taxes) over actual receipts for FY 2010 to "buy down" future income tax rates on individuals and corporations. The long-term goal was to get individual rates to zero, but the base corporate rate could not drop below 3.5 percent; an exception for rate reduction was provided when the select tax receipts in a given year fell below the previous year's level.[43] The Supplemental Note on H Sub SB 1 prepared by KLRD estimated that it would reduce individual and corporate income tax receipts by $135.9 million in FY 2012 and $603.5 million in FY 2013.

The senate's failure to pass H Sub for SB 1 in 2011 was a contributing factor cited by several key players in the 2012 decision in the house and the governor's office to pass the tax reform bill that eventually became law, even though it was much more expensive than desired. The thinking was that it may have been the only viable option to get any tax relief passed, even if it needed to be modified in subsequent years.

In preparation for the 2012 legislative session, the Brownback administration explored multiple options to cut taxes and spur job creation. The initial intent was to provide relief for all taxpayers but C-corporations weren't included in the final plan, and that was of their own choice. Former Revenue Secretary Nick Jordan said there were hundreds of millions in earned but unclaimed tax credits on the state books, so considerable compromise needed to be reached on their disposition in order to reduce the C-corporation tax rates and broaden the tax base. Jordan said, "We wanted to go to zero, no corporate income tax eventually, but those with large tax credits wanted to keep them. So we said [the current rate structure] is going to stay."

Governor Brownback's tax-relief plan was developed by Kansas Department of Revenue Secretary Nick Jordan and his staff. State Budget Director Steve Anderson, University of Kansas economist Dr. Arthur Hall, and former advisor to President Reagan Dr. Arthur Laffer were consulted but the plan was designed by KDOR staff.

The long-term goal was to get everyone to zero, and by "long-term" it was understood it would take much more time than an eight-year term. The short-term goal, according to Nick Jordan, was to "get individual rates as low as we could then. And somewhere along the way—and I'm being credited with this although I'm not sure I was the one—I said to the governor, 'Well, if you're gonna take someone to zero, let's think about small business. Those are the job creators.'" That started the conversation about getting pass-through businesses that are taxed as individuals (proprietors, partnerships, Sub-s corporations, and limited liability corporations, where the income from those entities is "passed through" to the individual owners) to zero income tax. Jordan said it was the goal of the Tax Division to provide tax relief in "administratively the best way to do it," and that led to proposing to immediately take those businesses to zero rather than to do so gradually.

Governor Brownback said his initial focus was only on cutting marginal tax rates for individuals, but then Nick Jordan showed him the economic modeling on removing income tax on pass-through businesses. "And, so, I was looking at the economic models and going, 'Boom, man, that baby just shoots up job creation,' which was our target. That was our primary focus, job creation. It wasn't revenue, it was job creation, because we were anemic on job creation. We were behind on national averages on small business creation. Our turn rate on small businesses was terrible . . . we just weren't creating enough and we were losing way too many of them."

Heavy Dependency on Small Business

Table 5: Tax Year 2015 Pass-Through Income (millions)				
Net Income Level	Tax Returns			Business Income
	Number	% Total	Cumulative	
Loss reported	95,771	28.6%	28.6%	$ (1,692.3)
Zero to $25,000	179,194	53.4%	82.0%	$ 1,163.5
$25,000 to $50,000	26,013	7.8%	89.7%	$ 920.0
$50,000 to $75,000	11,192	3.3%	93.1%	$ 684.2
$75,000 to $100,000	5,827	1.7%	94.8%	$ 503.6
$100,000 to $250,000	11,245	3.4%	98.2%	$ 1,730.6
$250,000 to $500,000	3,727	1.1%	99.3%	$ 1,285.4
$500,000 to$1,000,000	1,527	0.5%	99.7%	$ 1,048.7
Over $1,000,000	905	0.3%	100.0%	$ 2,383.4
	335,401	100.0%		$ 8,027.1
Source: Kansas Department of Revenue				

Jordan said they believed that most small businesses would be those with less than $75,000 in net income and they were right. The most recently available data as this book went to press (Tax Year 2015) shows 93 percent of pass-through entities had less than $75,000 in net income. Most of the net income, however, was consistently concentrated in companies with net income greater than $250,000, and that fueled criticism that the pass-through exemption really only helped "the wealthy."

The largest tax savings went to the more profitable companies but the benefits to the less profitable were also significant. A steady stream of small-business owners testified during legislative hearings on proposals to eliminate the exemption that it had provided them with much-needed capital to buy some equipment, catch up on deferred maintenance, hire or at least retain workers, and in some cases, keep the doors open.

There is also a significant but unseen economic value to states in eliminating (or greatly reducing) the tax burden because it encourages risk-taking that leads to new businesses being formed.

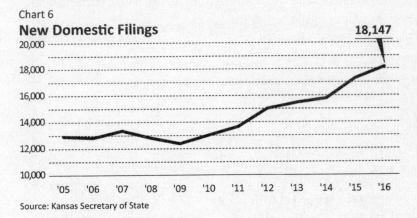

Chart 6
New Domestic Filings

18,147

Source: Kansas Secretary of State

Kansas experienced a significant uptick in new domestic (Kansas-based) business filings with implementation of the pass-through exemption.[44] Media and others routinely wrote off the increase as likely due to new organizations being formed to take advantage of the pass-through exemption, but that wasn't the case. The Kansas Secretary of State's Office said companies that restructured (whether from a C-corp to one of several pass-through entities or vice versa) would not be included in New Domestic Filings.[45] The business filings report also does not include proprietorships, so a W-2 wage earner that converted to 1099 status as a proprietor would also not cause the new domestic filings totals to change.

Setting a record for new business filings is much more important than mere "bragging rights." As explained in *A Thousand Flowers Blooming—Understanding Job Growth and the Kansas Tax Reforms*, "Job growth [in Kansas] is critically dependent on new business formation. Several studies have found that start-ups and young firms drive overall job creation.[46] A key academic study found that 'firm births contributed substantially to both gross and net job creation.'"[47] To see how this has played out over time in Kansas, Chart 7 below shows the trend of total job creation and jobs created excluding those created by new establishments from 1977 through 2014, the most current data available from the Census Bureau.

Chart 7

Kansas Private Job Growth

Only 2 years of growth without jobs from new establishments.

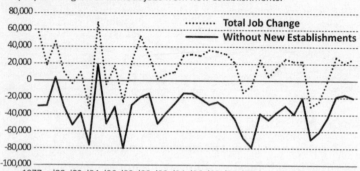

Source: U.S. Census

Census defines an establishment as "a single physical location where business is conducted or where services or industrial operations are performed;" they define a firm as "a business organization consisting of one or more domestic establishments that were specified under common ownership or control, with the firm and the establishment being the same for single-establishment firms." For example, new establishments could be a new bio-tech startup, a proprietor opening a new restaurant, or even a new Walmart location.

The authors drive home the importance of jobs from new establishments in Kansas and throughout the United States, referencing research pioneered by Dr. Hall. "In Kansas, with the exception of 1979 and 1984, the total number of jobs created would actually have been negative if not for the job creation from new establishments." Noting that this phenomenon is not unique to Kansas, the authors report that "the United States would have not had a single year of positive job growth [between 1997 and 2014] if not for jobs created by new establishments."

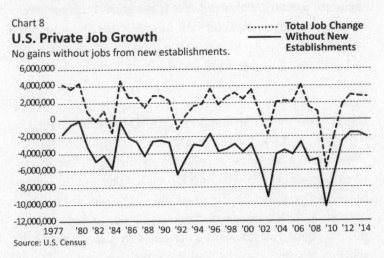

Chart 8
U.S. Private Job Growth
No gains without jobs from new establishments.

········ **Total Job Change**
—— **Without New Establishments**

Source: U.S. Census

The economic dynamism reflected in the data also creates broad implications for economic development policy. In his 2010 paper entitled *Embracing Dynamism*, Hall's conclusions universally apply to all cities, counties, and states. "The goal of embracing dynamism is simply stated: Create the conditions necessary to induce as much commercial experimentation as possible on Kansas soil. Proper execution of the embracing dynamism strategy will create an environment where all manner of people—inside and outside the state—feel motivated to commit their time and treasure to Kansas soil. The policy challenge centers on promoting dynamism by establishing a business environment that induces business birth and expansion without bias related to the size or type of business.

"Every business matters. Embracing dynamism starts with a change in vision—the state government of Kansas should abandon its prevailing policy of the State as an active investor in targeted businesses or industries and instead adopt the policy vision of the State as a caretaker of a competitive platform that seeks to induce as much commercial experimentation as possible. This vision implies the state government need not commit scarce resources to the enormously difficult task of predicting the outcome of competition if it focuses on the much more manageable task of creating the platform on which the competition takes place."[48]

Capping the Pass-Through Exemption Might Have Saved It

Reflectively, Nick Jordan thinks the pass-through exemption might have been acceptable to the public if it had been capped at $75,000 or $100,000. "The public probably would've said, 'OK, let's take care of the small-business person.' But that image that the media and everyone else put out there, that this was a bunch of fat cats, so to speak, the rich business owners, and then they got confused with corporate."

There's actually data that demonstrates the confusion as well as Jordan's belief that the public would have supported a partial exemption for pass-through businesses with low income. The Docking Institute of Public Affairs at Fort Hays State University published its annual Statewide Public Opinion Survey in May 2017, which found only 26 percent of Kansans said taxes should be increased on small business; 29 percent said small business taxes should remain the same and 46 percent said taxes should decrease.[49]

But Question 14 of that same survey found 70 percent of Kansans also believed the pass-through exemption should be eliminated, confirming Jordan's comment about many citizens being confused on which businesses were getting a tax break. Once again, insufficient messaging coupled with media opposition to tax relief left most citizens misinformed.

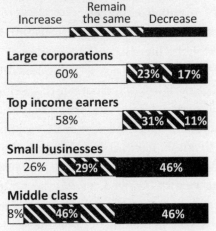

Docking Survey Figure 9:

Should taxes increase, remain the same or decrease for each of the following groups?

Increase | Remain the same | Decrease

Large corporations
60% | 23% | 17%

Top income earners
58% | 31% | 11%

Small businesses
26% | 29% | 46%

Middle class
8% | 46% | 46%

Source: Docking Institute at Fort Hays State University

The notion that the tax cuts were hoped or intended to pay for themselves is yet another persistent myth. Howard Gleckman, a senior fellow at the Urban-Brookings Tax Policy Center at the Urban Institute, wrote in a *Forbes* guest column, "Once again we are testing the question: Can tax cuts pay for themselves?"[50] It was never the plan for the Kansas tax cuts to "pay for themselves," but that didn't stop tax-relief opponents from constructing that straw man argument in order to disparage the effort. Every legislative analysis of the tax-relief effort was done on a static basis, wherein the immediate impact of policy changes are reflected and no consideration is given to potential dynamic effects resulting from taxpayers' reaction to the policy change.

Interviews with those involved in the development of the Kansas plan confirmed there was no expectation of the 2012 tax cuts paying for themselves, or even coming close to doing so. Indeed, former State Budget Director Steve Anderson consistently warned legislators and the governor's administration that looming, long-term budget shortfalls would occur unless spending was brought in line with the intended revenue reductions.

Unrelated Economic Challenges

KDOR used dynamic scoring software from Regional Economic Models, Inc. (REMI) to predict the long-term economic effects of cutting taxes. Dynamic scoring predicts incremental gains or losses attributable to specific changes in policy based on structural relationships between economic indicators and the speed of economic responses. (Static scoring, on the other hand, assumes no reaction to change.) KDOR economist Michael Austin explained just one of the complicating factors involved, saying the tax plan "had a two-pronged and a lagged effect; the tax cut affected individuals (Real Disposable Income) and businesses (Production Costs). The lagged effect was that though the tax policy took effect in 2013, [the full impact of] tax effects weren't felt [on state revenues] until [fiscal years] 2014 and 2015."

Here's an extremely simplified explanation of the underlying basis of dynamic scoring on a tax reduction for individuals. Real disposable income is increased by the amount of the tax cut and a historically predictable portion of the increased real disposable income is spent on goods and services. Gradually, that increased economic activity prompts employers to purchase more inventory and/or hire more workers to meet the growing demand. Taxes are another cost of production to business, so dynamic scoring can relate lower production costs to lower prices for consumers and/or higher wages for employees. Over time, lower prices encourage more economic activity and thereby stimulate more economic growth.

Dynamic scoring predictions would be fairly reliable if only one variable changed (in this case, a tax cut), but that is rarely the case—and Kansas experienced a great deal of economic volatility unrelated to tax policy that would undermine the anticipated benefits of a tax cut.

Many of the Obamacare tax increases, mandates, and resultant increases in insurance premiums kicked in simultaneously with the Kansas tax cuts and more followed in the years to come. Quite a few pass-through business owners said the state income tax savings merely covered their higher tax and insurance costs related to Obamacare. This recap prepared by Americans for Tax Reform only includes the changes implemented between 2013 and 2016:[51]

1. [omitted]
2. Obamacare Individual Mandate Excise Tax (takes effect in Jan. 2014): Starting in 2014, anyone not buying "qualifying" health insurance—as defined by Obama-appointed HHS bureaucrats—must pay an income surtax according to the higher of the following:

	1 Adult	2 Adults	3+ Adults
2014	1% AGI/$95	1% AGI/$190	1% AGI/$285
2015	2% AGI/$325	2% AGI/$650	2% AGI/$975
2016	+2.5% AGI/$695	2.5% AGI/$1390	2.5% AGI/$2085

The Congressional Budget Office recently estimated that six million American families will be liable for the tax, and as Americans for Tax Reform has pointed out, 100 percent of Americans filing a tax return (140 million filers) will be forced to submit paperwork to the IRS showing they had "qualifying" health insurance for every month of the tax year. *Bill: PPACA; Page: 317–337*
3. Obamacare Employer Mandate Tax (takes effect Jan. 2014): If an employer does not offer health coverage, and at least one employee qualifies for a health tax credit, the employer must pay an additional non-deductible tax of $2,000 for all full-time employees.

Applies to all employers with 50 or more employees. If any employee actually receives coverage through the exchange, the penalty on the employer for that employee rises to $3,000. If the employer requires a waiting period to enroll in coverage of 30–60 days, there is a $400 tax per employee ($600 if the period is 60 days or longer). *Bill: PPACA; Page: 345–346.* Combined score of individual and employer mandate tax penalty: $65 billion/10 years.

4. Obamacare Surtax on Investment Income (Tax hike of $123 billion/takes effect Jan. 2013): Creation of a new, 3.8 percent surtax on investment income earned in households making at least $250,000 ($200,000 single). This would result in the following top tax rates on investment income: *Bill: Reconciliation Act; Page: 87–93*

	Capital Gains	Dividends	Other*
2011–2012	15%	15%	35%
2013+ (current law)	23.8%	43.4%	43.4%
2013+ (Obama budget)	23.8%	23.8%	43.4%

*Other unearned income includes (for surtax purposes) gross income from interest, annuities, royalties, net rents, and passive income in partnerships and Subchapter-S corporations. It does not include municipal bond interest or life insurance proceeds, since those do not add to gross income. It does not include active trade or business income, fair market value sales of ownership in pass-through entities, or distributions from retirement plans. The 3.8 percent surtax does not apply to non-resident aliens.

5. [omitted]

6. Obamacare Hike in Medicare Payroll Tax (Tax hike of $86.8 bil/takes effect Jan. 2013): Current law and changes:

	First $200,000 ($250,000 Married) Employer/Employee	All Remaining Wages Employer/Employee
Current Law	1.45%/1.45% 2.9% self-employed	1.45%/1.45% 2.9% self-employed
Obamacare Tax Hike	1.45%/1.45% 2.9% self-employed	1.45%/2.35% 3.8% self-employed

Bill: PPACA, Reconciliation Act; Page: 2000–2003; *87–93*

7–8. [omitted]

9. Obamacare Flexible Spending Account Cap—aka "Special Needs Kids Tax" (Tax hike of $13 bil/takes effect Jan. 2013): Imposes cap on FSAs of $2,500 (currently unlimited). Indexed to inflation after 2013. There is one group of FSA owners for whom this new cap will be particularly cruel and onerous: parents of special needs children. There are thousands of families with special needs children in the United States, and many of them use FSAs to pay for special needs education. Tuition rates at one leading school that teaches special needs children in Washington, D.C. (National Child Research Center) can easily exceed $14,000 per year. Under tax rules, FSA dollars can be used to pay for this type of special needs education. *Bill: PPACA; Page: 2,388–2,389*

10. Obamacare Tax on Medical Device Manufacturers (Tax hike of $20 bil/takes effect Jan. 2013): Medical device manufacturers 409,000 people in 12,000 plants across the country. This law imposes a new 2.3 percent excise tax on total sales, even if the respective company does not earn a profit. Exempts items retailing for <$100. *Bill: PPACA; Page: 1,980–1,986*

11. Obamacare "Haircut" for Medical Itemized Deduction from 7.5% to 10% of AGI (Tax hike of $15.2 bil/takes

effect Jan. 2013): Currently, those facing high medical expenses are allowed a deduction for medical expenses to the extent that those expenses exceed 7.5 percent of adjusted gross income (AGI). The new provision imposes a threshold of 10 percent of AGI. Waived for 65+ taxpayers in 2013–2016 only. *Bill: PPACA; Page: 1,994–1,995*

12. [omitted]
13. Obamacare elimination of tax deduction for employer-provided retirement Rx drug coverage in coordination with Medicare Part D (Tax hike of $4.5 bil/takes effect Jan. 2013) *Bill: PPACA; Page: 1,994*

14–16. [omitted]
17. Obamacare Tax on Health Insurers (Tax hike of $60.1 bil/takes effect Jan. 2014): Annual tax on the industry imposed relative to health insurance premiums collected that year. Phases in gradually until 2018. Fully imposed on firms with $50 million in profits. *Bill: PPACA; Page: 1,986–1,993*

18. Obamacare $500,000 Annual Executive Compensation Limit for Health Insurance Executives (Tax hike of $0.6 bil/takes effect Jan 2013). *Bill: PPACA; Page: 1,995–2,000*

19–21. [omitted]

Aerospace and aviation is very important to Kansas, with several major manufacturing facilities and related parts suppliers located primarily in Wichita, including Boeing, Spirit AeroSystems, Cessna, Beechcraft, and Bombardier Learjet. Unfortunately, global economic conditions and workforce relocations created havoc in the industry throughout the Kansas tax-cut effort. Boeing ended its eighty-five-year history in Wichita in the middle of 2014, moving work to Texas, Oklahoma, and Washington state.[52] Between 2012 and 2016, average annual employment in Aerospace Product and Parts

Table 6: 2012 Share of Private GDP		
Industry	U.S.	Kansas
Farms	1.1%	4.3%
Oil & gas extraction	1.9%	1.5%
Petroleum / coal mfg.	1.2%	3.5%
Other trans. equip. mfg.	0.8%	3.9%
Total	5.1%	13.2%
Source: Bureau of Econonmic Analysis		

Manufacturing dropped 8 percent,[53] and the loss of those jobs had a negative economic ripple effect, especially in the Wichita area. The Bureau of Economic Analysis reports Gross Domestic Product for Aerospace Product and Parts Manufacturing in the Other Transportation Equipment Manufacturing category, which accounted for 3.9 percent of the Kansas private sector GDP in 2012, but the national average was only 0.8 percent.[54]

Kansas is also more dependent on agriculture, where farms accounted for 4.3 percent of private GDP in 2012 versus the national average of 1.1 percent. Oil and gas extraction and petroleum refining is another outlier for Kansas, at a combined 5 percent of private GDP against a national average of 3.1 percent. On top of Obamacare and aerospace challenges, commodity prices for key agricultural products and oil dropped precipitously.

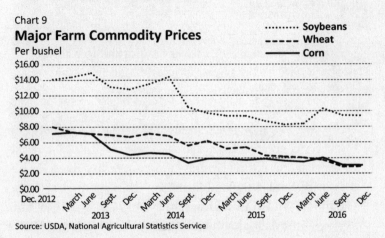

Chart 9
Major Farm Commodity Prices
Per bushel

········· Soybeans
- - - - - Wheat
——— Corn

Source: USDA, National Agricultural Statistics Service

Just as tax cuts went into effect in 2013, corn, wheat, and soybean prices began a slow decline that grew worse during 2014 and continued through 2015. Soybeans made a partial comeback in 2016, but corn and wheat continued to fall. By the end of 2016, corn had fallen 57 percent from $7.15 per bushel to just $3.05. Soybeans had fallen by a third, from $14.10 to $9.39 per bushel and wheat was hit the hardest, falling from $8.01 per bushel to $2.88—a drop of 64 percent.[55]

Farm income declined as prices fell. The Kansas Farm Management Association at Kansas State University reports average net income fell from $159,352 in 2012 to $140,356 in 2013 and then to $128,731 in 2014. The cumulative effect of commodity price declines decimated farm income over the following two years, with average net income of just $6,744 in 2015 and $43,161 in 2016.[56]

State Sales Tax Collections, Percent Change by County

The sales tax rate increased from 6.15% to 6.5% July 1, 2015, creating a total statewide 6.0% increase during July 2015-June 2016.

Fiscal-Year-to-Date 2016/2015 percent change (July 2015-June 2016)

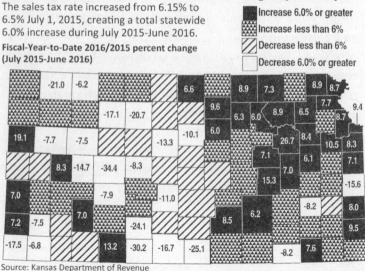

Source: Kansas Department of Revenue

Pass-through income for farms was exempt from income tax between 2013 and 2016 so income tax estimates weren't affected, but sales tax receipts were hit hard as the cutback on farm spending rippled throughout the economy, as shown on this map of state sales tax collections by county for FY 2016.[57] The state sales tax rate increased by 6 percent effective July 1, 2015, so collections should have increased by that amount. However, twenty western Kansas counties—home to much of the state's farmland—experienced declines of more than 6 percent and another thirteen counties had smaller declines. Only seven western Kansas counties experienced real growth in taxable retail sales and use tax activity.

Steep declines in oil prices also hurt much of the agricultural area in Kansas as there is considerable geographic overlap. The Cushing, Oklahoma, crude price hovered around $100 per barrel in late 2013 and early 2014 but fell below $50 by March 2015, and a year later was only at $38.[58] Natural gas fell 65 percent between March 2014 and March 2016 before beginning to recover.[59]

Chart 10
Cushing Oklahoma Crude Oil Future

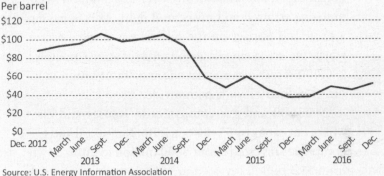

Source: U.S. Energy Information Association

A combination of price declines and related production cutbacks caused severance tax collections to plummet from $125.8 million in FY 2014 to just $22.4 million in FY 2016; collections improved a bit to $42.1 million in FY 2016 but still considerably contributed to state budget shortfalls.

The impact to the Kansas economy was also extensive, as explained in a white paper published by the Kansas Independent Oil & Gas Association (KIOGA).

To understand this better, let's look at capital expenditures (capex) which are *Funds used by companies to maintain or increase the scope of their operations.* This kind of spending is very good for an economy. It builds infrastructure, it creates jobs, and is an investment in the future. Companies make these investments because they believe they will get a good return on those investments. Unfortunately, when the price of oil crashes those investments become unprofitable and capex gets cut ($69.2 billion cut nationwide in 2015 and $89.6 billion cut in 2016). Kansas crude oil prices dropped below $20 per barrel in early 2016 as a global glut of production drastically dropped prices. The drop in crude oil prices triggered over 100 oil and gas producer bankruptcies across the nation since the beginning of 2015 that involve over $34.3 billion in cumulative secured and unsecured debt. This is having a profound impact on the oil and gas service sector where we are seeing large job cuts [of approximately] 250,000 direct industry layoffs and about 1 million indirect industry layoffs nationwide.

Many oil and gas companies in Kansas and elsewhere cut capex by 75–80% in 2016. Kansas oil and gas companies invested about $300 million in 2016, down from $1.3 billion invested in 2014. Kansas oil and gas companies have invested over $1 billion annually in 8 of the last 11 years. Companies have deferred well completions and many high-cost marginal wells are being temporarily shut-in. As a result, royalty payments to Kansas oil and gas royalty owners dropped by about $400 million in 2016.

In Kansas, much like the rest of the nation, some oil and gas service companies have laid off as much as 55–60% of their workforce and reduced wages by as much as 20–25% and some producers have laid off as much as 20–25% of their workforce. As a result, family income has dropped by about $341 million across Kansas. Direct oil and gas employment loss in Kansas since 2014 is over 3,100. When you add in indirect jobs, employment losses in the Kansas oil and gas industry jumps to over 6,100.[60]

By the way, the Kansas crude oil price mentioned in the KIOGA white paper is less than the open-market prices shown in Chart 10 because, according to KIOGA President Edward Cross, "Kansas common crude oil is a little lesser quality oil and produces less products per barrel than WTI and, as a result, is priced about $10–$11 per barrel less."

The Plan Comes Together

Legislators were certainly aware that Governor Brownback intended to cut taxes, but they weren't included in the plan design, and that would prove to be a messaging challenge. Having upfront buy-in from key legislators would have far better positioned those key legislators to vocally support and explain the plan to constituents; instead, only a few knew the plan and the rationale behind it well enough to comfortably discuss it. Opponents would seize on that uncertainly.

After much deliberation, Governor Brownback and his team settled on the following components, which were introduced in January 2012 in the house as HB 2560 and in the senate as SB 339, with all changes going into effect for the 2013 tax year:[61]

- Collapse the three-bracket structure for individual income taxes (3.5, 6.25, and 6.5 percent) to two brackets (3.0 percent and 4.9 percent).
- Exempt all non-wage business income that businesses would otherwise report from state individual income taxes (as reported by LLCs, S-Corps, and sole proprietorships on lines 12, 17, and 18 of the federal form 1040 individual income tax return).
- Eliminate all itemized deductions and tax credits for the individual income tax, except for the High Performance Incentive Program Tax Credit and Community Entrepreneurship Tax Credit.
- Eliminate the Learning Quest and Long Term Care subtraction modifications.
- Prohibit renters from qualifying for the Homestead Property Tax Refund Program.
- Eliminate the Food Sales Tax Rebate Program.
- Maintain the state retail sales and compensating use tax rates at 6.3 percent instead of allowing it to reduce to 5.7 percent on July 1, 2013, as required by current law, and adjust the transfer percentage to allow the same amount to go to the State Highway Fund as under current law.
- Repeal the current two-year severance tax exemption on new pool oil and gas wells, except for oil wells generating fifty barrels or fewer per day.

The governor's plan would have provided $352.2 million in net tax relief over the first five fiscal years. In March of 2012, the house Taxation Committee would amend the governor's plan and push the cost to just over $1 billion.

But in a battle of bare-knuckle politics, the left-leaning senate would soon multiply the impact of the governor's proposal by a factor of ten.

3

How Tax Relief Became Law

"No one should see how laws or sausages are made. To retain respect for sausages and laws, one must not watch them in the making. The making of laws, like the making of sausages, is not a pretty sight."

—Otto von Bismarck

Governor Brownback campaigned on lowering taxes, but he first publicly announced his policy initiative to flatten and simplify the tax code during his 2012 State of the State Address.[62] His ambitious proposal would eliminate the highest income tax bracket and reduce individual income tax rates for all Kansans while eliminating individual state income taxes on income reported on federal tax return Schedules C, E, and F—small businesses known as pass-through entities (proprietorships, partnerships, Subchapter S corporations, and limited liability corporations that elect to be taxed as individuals), rents, royalties, and farm income.

To make it work, he proposed "leveling the playing field by eliminating income tax credits, deductions, and exemptions." He proposed capping the amount of state revenue growth to 2 percent, and using any extra to further reduce individual and corporate income tax rates in subsequent years, which became known as the "march to zero" income tax plan.

The negative response from lawmakers was swift.

In the Democratic response to Brownback's speech, Kansas House Minority Leader Paul Davis said, "Brownback's proposal to eliminate the state income tax won't be much of a tax cut at all. It will simply shift the tax burden from corporations and our wealthiest citizens to those with the least means to pay."[63]

The tax package legislators eventually passed resembled sausage without a casing. What may have started as sincere efforts to adopt a tax plan with which most could live ended with a negotiation stalemate and a "nuclear option" that eventually became law. The final 2012 product contained a $4.5 billion tax cut through 2018[64] and became a budget and tax solution that wouldn't hold together over the long term.

The Governor Announces His Plan

Assisted by Lt. Gov. Jeff Colyer and State Budget Director Steve Anderson, Brownback introduced his tax plan to a joint meeting of house and senate tax committee members the second week of January. In addition to keeping a portion of sales tax that was set to sunset, the original legislation included a number of "pay-fors" that were designed to simplify and streamline the tax code by eliminating itemized deductions. The pay-fors eliminated the following tax credits:

- Abandoned well plugging credit;
- Adoption credit;
- Agritourism liability insurance credit;
- Alternative fuel tax credit;
- Angel investor credit;
- Assistive technology contribution credit;
- Child and dependent care credit;
- Child day care assistance credit;
- Community service contribution credit;
- Disabled access credit;
- Earned income credit;
- Environmental compliance credit;
- Historic preservation credit;
- Individual development account credit;
- Law enforcement training center credit;

- National Guard employer health credit;
- Research and development credit;
- Single city port authority credit;
- Small employer health benefit plan credit;
- Swine facility improvement credit;
- Telecommunications credit;
- Temporary assistance to families contribution credit;
- Venture capital and local seed capital credits.[65]

Separately, Brownback proposed adding $60 million to the state budget for social services and healthcare programs to alleviate concerns about eliminating the Earned Income Tax Credit.

In total, Brownback's tax proposal would have reduced revenue by $89.9 million in the first year and $352.2 million over five years. Out of the gate, lawmakers questioned the pay-fors, or the elements of the policy necessary to balance slightly slimmer revenues with expenditures. Democrats immediately warned that eliminating the home mortgage interest deduction would mean lower-income Kansans footing the cost of government. The day after the full rollout of the proposal, the Home Builders Association and real estate associations said eliminating the mortgage deduction would damage the state's economy.

"Mortgage interest deduction is certainly a cornerstone of homeownership and it strengthens communities and it puts people to work," Sarah Corless, a lobbyist for the HBA, told the *Kansas City Star*.[66]

The mortgage interest deduction was one of the first to draw ire from lawmakers; the angst from Republican and Democratic legislators began appearing in Kansas newspapers long before legislative committees hosted hearings on it. The *Kansas City Star* reported a week after Brownback's address that his tax plan "would hit poor the hardest."[67] That was the headline.

The mortgage interest deduction and the earned income tax credit were two of more than a dozen deductions Brownback recommended scrapping in exchange for reducing income tax rates. Both were highly unpopular from the start.

For as much ink as has since been spilled about Kansas's 2012 tax reform, little was written about tax and budget issues during the 2012 session. Other issues in the Kansas legislature dominated coverage of the legislative session. The Kansas legislative session is supposed to last ninety days, running from mid-January to late May with a few breaks in between. It was an election year, but even that was a backdrop to stories about reapportionment and school finance.

Brownback wasn't alone in proposing tax cuts. The question on tax cuts became: Which taxes and in return for which deductions? The governor and a conservative majority in the house appeared to be moving in the same direction, but the senate, with its moderate Republican leadership, was pulling the opposite way.

Brownback's tax proposal was introduced as SB 339 in the senate and as HB 2560 in the house. The senate Committee on Assessment and Taxation and house Taxation Committee would both hold several days of hearings.

House Committee Hearings

The house hearings ran for several hours over two days, February 8 and February 9. Forty people testified in person or provided written testimony on the proposal. It was a mixed bag. The Brownback administration's Nick Jordan, secretary of revenue, testified in support of the legislation,[68] as did representatives from the National Federation of Independent Business,[69] the Kansas Bankers Association,[70] Kansas Policy Institute, and a few business owners.

The Kansas Association of Realtors,[71] the Kansas Association of School Boards,[72] and the Kansas National Education

Association[73] testified against the legislation. They were joined by the Wichita city government. Chambers of Commerce in the state didn't speak with one voice. The Kansas Chamber of Commerce[74] and the Wichita Metro Chamber offered testimony[75] in support, while the Salina Area Chamber and Kansas City Chamber[76] offered neutral testimony.

Jason Watkins, director of governmental relations at the Wichita Chamber, compared Kansas to Oklahoma in his testimony. He said Oklahoma led the nation in GDP in 2009 with a 6.6 percent increase, while Kansas declined by 1.1 percent.

"Over the last decade, Oklahoma has increased its population while Kansas has seen a decrease. This is a pattern we actually see nationwide. People are voting with their feet; leaving high-tax states and moving to low-tax states. Low-tax states are outpacing high-tax states in income, population growth, and growth in state receipts," Watkins told the committee. "However, people for the most part, are not moving in an effort to avoid taxes; they are seeking jobs and personal prosperity. Simply put, people are going where the work is, and the work is in states with low taxes that are thereby attracting employers."[77]

Kansas Policy Institute supported "the overall concept of tax reform" and stated that HB 2560 had "some unique and attractive aspects that provide a good starting point for a discussion of tax reform."[78] KPI circumstantially supported exempting non-wage pass-through income from state income tax, citing "current economic and long-term budgetary conditions," but it opposed the changes to income tax deductions, Earned Income Tax Credits, and Food Sales Tax Rebates as well as not allowing the retail sales tax rate to decline as in statute; 2009 simulations released by the Department of Revenue showed those with Adjusted Gross Incomes below $25,000 would have seen a net increase in tax burden.[79]

In his neutral testimony, Dennis Lauver of the Salina Area Chamber of Commerce, offered support for the pass-through exemption, but voiced concerns that lowering income tax rates would damage the PEAK program, a business incentive that allows some employers to keep the share of state taxes they pay for employees.

"Without a replacement funding source, legislators should avoid voting to cut a proven job creating program—especially in this economy," Lauver told the committee.[80]

Several organizations voiced concern about the elimination of different deductions. For example, Sister Therese Bangert testified on behalf of the Sisters of Charity. She worried that eliminating the earned income tax credit would be a hardship for some families.

"In our Sister of Charity ministries in Kansas we serve through our hospitals and clinics many of the parents who receive this credit. Also, many of these parents work with us in our clinics and hospitals. Policies that protect and support them and their families are important to us," she told the committee.[81]

Media coverage of the hearings was sparse for what would become, a few years later, a major news story not just in Kansas, but throughout the country. Searches of the archives for the *Kansas City Star* and the *Wichita Eagle*, the largest daily papers in the state, don't turn up any stories between February 8 and February 10, 2012, about the house hearings, and no media signed in on hearing guest lists.[82] (Signing in isn't a requirement for attendance, though a sign-in sheet is passed around legislative committee hearings.)

After two days of hearings, the legislation languished in committee until mid-March when it was forwarded to the full house. House leadership has broad discretion to decide which bills passed out of committees are debated on the floor by the entire body, colloquially known as moving a bill "above the line." The governor's bill in the house died on the calendar, never making it above the line.

Senate Hearings on the Governor's Plan

The senate Committee on Assessment and Taxation opened hearings on the governor's plan, SB 339, a week later. Former Senate President Steve Morris said the senate Committee on Assessment and Taxation was one of the most conservative senate committees. That was by design, he explained in a 2017 interview.

"Between the moderate Republicans and Democrats, [the senate] had more than enough votes to kill or pass legislation," Morris said. "Normally, we would be on the same page."

Senate leadership assigns committee chairs and membership.

"We wanted to have the majority of committee chairs with more moderate Republicans," Morris said. "Because we were in a moderate recession at the time, we didn't think the tax committee would do anything dramatic. The majority (of the committee) ended up more conservative, because we didn't have anywhere else to put them. We thought it was a good idea at the time, but later it came back to bite us."

Many of the same individuals and organizations who offered testimony to the house committee offered similar testimony before the senate Committee on Assessment and Taxation.

Kent Eckles, then vice president of governmental affairs at the Kansas Chamber of Commerce, told the committee it is possible to lower income tax rates while increasing revenue. According to the book, *Rich States, Poor States*, states without income taxes increased their general fund spending by 54 percent between 2000 and 2008 while the rest of the country increased general fund expenditures by only 46 percent, Eckles said.

"How is that possible? Their increased economic activity allowed them to spend more because their private sector grew," he told the committee.[83]

The school lobby shared its concerns about education funding. Mark Tallman, the associate director for advocacy for the Kansas Association of School Boards, said a provision in the bill limiting the annual general spending increases to no greater than 2 percent per year to reduce income tax rates would reverse the state's commitment to education funding.

"We do not believe the people of Kansas today support reducing the state's role in funding that system and transferring the burden to local revenues," Tallman told the committee.[84]

That was one of several provisions that would eventually be stripped from the bill. The legislation sat for another month before the senate Committee on Assessment and Taxation took it up again. In the meantime, house Republicans announced their own plan to cut taxes.

A Republican House Plan

Before a single hearing occurred on Brownback's tax proposal, house Republicans announced their own tax plan, in HB 2747. The Kansas House was a decidedly conservative place in 2012. There were ninety-two Republicans in the 125-member house, and then Speaker Mike O'Neal said a solid seventy-six were conservatives.

O'Neal told the *Star* the house plan was a "prudent approach" in which the state ended the year with cash reserves.[85]

The house plan sought to lower income taxes by ratcheting down the individual income tax rate when revenues exceeded 2 percent growth. It would keep three tax brackets and reduce rates in each. However, the middle and bottom rates would be reduced at an accelerated rate with a goal of eventually reaching zero. The house Republican proposal would phase-in the LLC exemption, making those companies with profits less than $100,000 exempt from income taxes from 2013 to 2015. In 2016, pass-through companies earning less than $250,000 would be exempt. Beginning in 2018, all pass-through entities would be exempt from taxes. Perhaps most importantly from a political perspective, the payers in the lowest income tax bracket—$0 to $25,000—would pay $11 less per-capita under the house Republican proposal. They'd pay $156 more under the governor's plan.

The house plan allowed the sales tax rate to dip from 6.3 percent to 5.7 percent. It also kept a number of tax credits and deductions, including the home mortgage interest deduction—already a source of contention in the governor's proposal. It didn't eliminate the earned income tax credit, but reduced it beginning in 2014. The bill would return retail sales tax to the General Fund that was statutorily transferred to the state highway fund to partially offset the revenue decline initially. Like the governor's plan, the house proposal eliminated taxes on pass-through entities.[86]

"We're hoping the governor's vision, our vision, and ultimately, the senate's vision will be that we all reach the same destination," O'Neal said in 2012.[87]

As introduced in HB 2747, state revenues would be short $41.7 million in FY 2013 and the five-year revenue decline would be $1.06 billion.[88]

The house Committee on Taxation hosted two days of hearings on the proposal in mid-February. Many of the entities, individuals, and organizations that offered testimony in hearings on the governor's plan returned to the hearings on the house Republican plan. Some sang a different tune. For example, Luke Bell, the vice president for the Kansas Association of Realtors, testified in opposition to the governor's proposal, but he lent KAR's support for the house plan.

"Unlike the other comprehensive income tax proposals that are currently being discussed by the Kansas legislature, HB 2747 provides comprehensive, equitable, and meaningful tax relief to all Kansans and does not increase the tax burden on a particular group or group of Kansas taxpayers to provide relief for all Kansans," Bell's written testimony reads.[89]

Several people expressed concerns about using sales tax funding to buy down income tax rates instead of being used for highway funding as conceived in 2010 legislation that increased sales taxes by 1 cent, a portion of which was set to expire in 2013.

Barbara Rankin, acting secretary for the Kansas Department of Transportation, warned that delaying state highway funds would prevent KDOT from maintaining current project schedules.[90] The Kansas League of Municipalities said the plan "raids" the highway fund.

Kansas Policy Institute, which previously had offered testimony in support of the governor's plans, testified neutral on the bill, though Kansas Policy Institute said using highway funds "makes sense, as we believe there is a much greater need for that money to be used for tax reduction than to expand an already excellent highway system. However, there are some aspects of HB 2747 that we find troubling."[91] KPI warned that the reduction in EITC credits in 2014 meant the lower income bracket had a higher tax liability in year two of the plan.

Others argued, once again, against the provision to exempt passive income.

"Let me first point out that HB 2747, just like the earlier bill, also exempts purely passive investment income that likely won't create any further Kansas jobs. An example is a shopping center in Lawrence in which I own a small percent," said Robert Vancrum, legislative policy and government affairs consultant for the Greater Kansas City Chamber of Commerce. "There will never be employees since the manager got his interest for operating the business. It appears the bill also exempts payments to Kansas investors from out-of-state partnerships. If the focus is on creating jobs, the exemption should be to an active trade or business that employs someone."[92]

A week later, the house committee used a parliamentary procedure to strip a bill already approved by the senate and replace it with an amended version of the house Republican tax plan. The new bill would be known as H Substitute for SB 177. The procedure, known as a "gut-and-go," allowed house lawmakers to skip a requirement for the full senate to vet the bill. Once passed by the house, it could be sent back to the chamber of origin where the senate could accept it as changed, negotiate terms acceptable to house and senate members in a conference committee, or vote to kill the bill by agreeing to disagree.

A senate committee later would use a similar procedure to place the governor's tax proposal into a bill previously passed by the house, HB 2117. On March 14, the senate Committee on Assessment and Taxation moved on the governor's plan. By amendment, committee members removed the portion of the bill eliminating the earned income tax credit, removed language that would limit the growth of general funding to 2 percent, and reinstated some of the tax credits including the historic tax credit and the community service tax credit. In short, the committee removed some of the pay-fors in the governor's bill.

Minutes later, the committee stripped the original language in HB 2117, a bill passed by the house in 2011 and never adopted by the senate. The senate committee replaced the text of HB 2117 with the new language of an amended SB 339, Brownback's tax proposal.

House Substitute for SB 177

A day earlier, the full house debated the Republican house plan, H Substitute for SB 177. During house debate, members amended the plan to increase general fund spending growth from 2 percent to 3 percent before triggering additional income tax reductions. House members also eliminated some tax credits, while adding back a tax credit for some taxpayers who relocated to rural Kansas from high unemployment counties, and repealed the sunset of a historic site tax credit.

Once it passed the full house on March 14, the senate had options. Members could decide to concur with the bill as amended, adopting the legislation; or not concur and decide to negotiate with the house for an agreement to bring to both chambers for an up or down vote. The senate did not concur with the plan. Instead, the full body adopted an amended version of the Brownback plan with some of the pay-fors removed.

A Tie Means Failure

A senate-amended version of the governor's tax proposal, now deemed Senate Sub HB 2117, reached the senate floor on March 20. The full senate amended it further. In a 2017 interview with this book's authors, Governor Brownback said senate members added poison pills that removed all of the pay-fors in an effort to kill it. He believes they bumped the costs and sweetened the tax cuts, so they could be on record voting for a tax cut on a bill no one thought would ever see the light of day as law.

On the floor, senators adopted amendments to drop a recommendation to maintain the sales tax rate of 6.3 percent, allowing it to drop to 5.7 percent. (During the same session, the senate killed a proposed amendment to lower the sales tax rate even further to 5.3 percent.[93]) They approved an amendment to keep all of the itemized tax deductions, and adopted another amendment to increase the standard deduction for joint tax filers from $6,000 to $9,000.[94] The end result was a bill that would garner a $231 million shortfall in year one, and a whopping $4.5 billion shortfall throughout the six-year period ending in 2018.[95]

Former Senate President Steve Morris said several senators thought the mortgage interest deduction and the charitable contribution deductions were important to Kansans—no matter what ultimately happened with the legislation.

"Those two things made the fiscal impact worse," he recalled. It nearly died with a dead-even senate vote of 20–20.[96] Morris voted against the bill, but he would vote in favor of the legislation when the senate reconsidered it a few hours later.

David Kensinger, who was then the governor's chief of staff, is convinced the tie vote was intentional.

"The senate took out the 'pay-fors' one-by-one. Mortgage deduction. Sales tax. Everyone who is working against the governor gets to vote for a tax break. The intent was to make the bill unworkable," Kensinger said. "That's the perfidy of what the senate leadership was doing to kill the bill."

There is no tie breaker in the Kansas Senate. The legislation flat lined, but the senate moved to reconsider the legislation a few hours later. Morris said that immediately following the tie vote, his assistant told him the governor wanted to speak with him.

"He pleaded and pleaded and pleaded for us to reconsider," Morris said. "He went on to say that he knew we couldn't do that. It would bankrupt the state . . . it was terrible public policy, and it would never become law. But he had to have something to go to conference with, because it was towards the end of the session and there were no other tax bills around."

Morris says he voted in support of the legislation the second time as a favor to the governor, because the governor promised the tax cut would be significantly reduced before he signed it.

Five years later Kansas City columnist Steve Kraske wrote about that fateful meeting of Morris and Brownback between the senate's tie vote and a second vote to reconsider, "Brownback doesn't recall it that way. But it's hard to imagine any other reason why Morris, a moderate, would sign off on such a huge cut absent that promise."[97]

Kensinger says that's garbage; the Governor's Office played hard ball. Two of the twenty who voted against the amended governor's tax plan were interested in other legislative items they hoped to see pass during the 2012 session. Kensinger will not say which lawmakers or what pieces of legislation they discussed, but Kensinger called a few legislators to the Governor's Office.

"I made it very clear to them if the governor's priorities didn't advance, their priorities weren't going to advance," Kensinger said.

He said those senators told Morris they wanted to reconsider the amended governor's tax plan.

"Steve Morris was going to lose a motion to reconsider later that afternoon," Kensinger said. "Knowing he was going to lose, Morris released his caucus. Nine Republicans that voted against it in the morning, voted for it that afternoon."

Morris, along with nine other Republicans switched their votes on the second attempt at passing HB 2117. It passed 29–11.

After the senate passed the tax plan, Morris said it was "unworkable."

"It will be a difficult process for those in the conference committee to come up with something that will pass muster," Morris told the *Star*.[98]

Democrats also didn't see that particular plan coming together. Senate Minority Leader Anthony Hensley said the bill passing the senate was the result of Brownback's "backdoor arm twisting."

Hensley added, "The plan we're left with is a five-year, $3.7 billion plan that will shift the tax burden onto middle class families and seniors living on fixed incomes to the detriment of public education and property tax relief."[99]

Republicans weren't enamored with it either. Former Speaker O'Neal said he understood why the senate didn't want that plan.

"I didn't want it either, to be perfectly honest," O'Neal said. "Because it didn't have the 'pay-fors,' you'd really have to crunch the budget tight the next year, which didn't happen, but we're getting ahead ourselves."

By the end of the day on March 21, a separate comprehensive tax plan had passed each chamber via gut-and-go procedures. The senate-amended versions of the governor's plan (Senate Sub HB 2117 and the house Republican plan (House Sub SB 177) were sent to conference committees, where three house members and three senate members were tasked with negotiating terms of one plan or the other.

The house could pass the "poisoned" version of Brownback's plan by concurring with the senate's bill, or the senate could do the same by concurring with the house Republican plan, or the chambers could reach a solution through the conference committee process.

Dual Filibusters

Instead, both pieces of legislation just languished.

"It just sits there for the rest of the legislative session," Brownback recalled. "We're trying to get the house to pass the senate's, but they won't because it's a big tax cut. But [the house] can't get the senate to do anything different. . . . It's going back and forth until finally one morning, we started hearing rumors."

The rumor was that the senate was going to adopt an agree-to-disagree motion on the conference committee of the house bill, and then refuse to re-appoint a new conference committee, effectively killing the Republican house plan.

That, Brownback said, made the house mad, and the house still had another tool in its arsenal. Members could concur with the "poisoned" senate bill, effectively passing tax reform.

"[The house] probably wouldn't have passed that bill if they hadn't gotten mad," Brownback said.

On May 9, the senate set to work attempting to kill the Republican house plan with a motion to agree to disagree on the senate floor. Meanwhile, the house was attempting to concur with the senate bill.

"There got to be a race, which in the legislature racing is— neither body works fast—it's like a turtle race is what you'd compare it to," Brownback said.

Morris described the start of the dueling filibusters differently.

He said the day the conference committee report went to the senate floor, "the governor asked the house to concur with what we passed—what he told us would never become law. While we were debating a revised conference committee report, the house ultimately passed that concur. At that point it was a done deal. The governor obviously went back on his word."

Both chambers worked feverishly. In the senate, house allies attempted to keep the clock running on a motion to agree to disagree, while moderates in the house attempted to keep the clock running on a motion to concur with the senate plan.

O'Neal thought it was a battle the house would lose, because there are 125 members in his chamber and only forty senate members.

"And under our rules, once we get to the vote, each member has up to a minute to explain their vote," O'Neal said.

An early call of the question ended debate, but house moderates were running out the clock explaining their votes. O'Neal was looking for an opportunity to close the roll.

House members push buttons on their desks to light up a board. When and if the lights went dark for any moment, O'Neal could make his move.

"There was a small lapse in time where there was no light on," O'Neal recalled. And the house Speaker called the roll.

One representative came out of his seat, and the sergeant-at-arms had to stop him.

"He wanted to kill me," O'Neal said. "He wanted to cause me physical harm."

It was over. Once the legislation reached the governor's desk, Brownback would have ten days to sign it, veto it, or let it become law without his signature. In the meantime, the senate and house could continue negotiations on the other, more preferable plan.

Brownback says senate leadership came to his office asking him to veto the legislation.

Morris contends, however, that Brownback promised the bill would never become law on the day the senate passed it.

"They won't tell me what they'll pass," Brownback said of senate leadership. "So I'm left with the option of either vetoing the bill because it's too big, and not having any promise of any tax cut, or signing a bill that's much larger than I proposed."

Brownback issued a public statement, asking lawmakers to compromise on the other bill. They had ten days.

"As with all bills approved by the Kansas legislature, I will carefully review and consider HB 2117. It would create tens of thousands of new jobs and combined with spending restraint, will help to reverse a lost decade of declining employment," Brownback said. "I am prepared to sign the bill, but I encourage Kansas legislators to continue their work on reforming our state's tax policy and to consider some of the alternatives I proposed in my original pro-growth tax reform to offset the cost."[100]

Still, Morris said the senate brought several proposals to

conference committee. Minutes of what occurred in conference committee don't exist, but Morris recalled the senate
offering suggestions for a more reasonable tax cut. Instead,
Morris said the house negotiators only offered solutions very
similar to what had already passed.

O'Neal said the goal of passing the other bill was simply for
leverage in the negotiations for the house Republican plan.
He recalled house negotiators offering all kinds of goodies
trying to get the senate to agree to the house Republican plan.

"I was basically giving the conference committee Christ-
mas tree ornaments to get them to go along with it," O'Neal
said.

For example, he offered $45 million in property tax re-
lief and a proposal to add $50 million in additional school
funding without weighting it. Three senators who were
likely opposed to any tax-relief proposal hailed from Johnson
County, which would have benefitted immensely from both
proposals.

"[The senate] turned every single one of them down,"
O'Neal recalled, "with the most conservative people in the
building throwing money at the schools and the most moderate people in the building turning it down."

Morris said he had regular conversations with the governor about school finance throughout the 2012 session.
Morris said he was concerned that schools were being short-
changed, and there was a pending lawsuit. He said those
discussions fell on deaf ears.

"The next week, I'd have the same conversation as if I'd
never talked to him before," Morris recalled. "It was like
Groundhog's Day."

The governor's staff continued advocating for the conference committee to reach a compromise. State Budget
Director Steve Anderson said lawmakers had two "beautiful
choices," as he urged house Republicans to consider endors-
ing the plan under negotiations.[101]

"It's kind of like the Miss America contest," Anderson told Republicans during a caucus meeting. "You have two beautiful options, but the one I would put the crown on would be the conference committee report."

Meanwhile, O'Neal said day one, day two, day three, passed. And then day four and five passed with no movement.

"Frankly, we would have done just about anything," he recalled. "We had such an aggressive plan on the governor's desk that it wouldn't have taken much to please [the house]."

The governor issued a public ultimatum on May 16, a few days after the house won the battle of the filibusters.

"In regards to reforming our state's tax policy, either send me the bill that came out of the conference committee last week, or I am going to sign HB 2117 when it arrives on my desk," Brownback said in a statement.[102]

The senate called Brownback's bluff. On May 18, the senate, by a narrow vote, of 18–21, decided not to consider the conference committee compromise.

Still, Brownback was anguished about signing the bill.

"The fiscal note was much higher than I had proposed and man, I chewed on that, prayed on that for about as long of period of time as I had," Brownback recalled.

O'Neal nudged him.

"He almost didn't sign it," the former house Speaker said. "My guilty secret is, I leaned on him hard to fulfill the promise that he made to our caucus, that if we couldn't come to an agreement, he would sign it."

Brownback said he ultimately decided the people could be trusted with their own money.

"I will put my money with the people more than the government any day, and that's what I ultimately came down with," he said. "This is letting the people have more of their own money, and we will work our way through."

Brownback publicly announced he would sign HB 2117 on May 18.

"It is unfortunate that the Kansas Senate has refused even to debate a tax compromise bill that would have provided Kansans tax relief," his statement read. "However, strengthening the Kansas economy cannot wait. We will have pro-growth tax reform in Kansas this year that will create tens of thousands of jobs and make our state the best place in America to start and grow a small business."[103]

Making It Work

"I regret that we didn't get a compromise, but I don't regret that it became law," O'Neal said, admitting he would do it again.

After the final gavel sounded on what would become known as the Brownback Tax Reform, Speaker O'Neal walked through the Capitol to his office.

"I was physically and emotionally drained," the former Speaker recalled. An attorney, O'Neal said he's tried several high-stress lawsuits, but he never felt as stressed as he did after he hit that gavel on HB 2117.

In the hall, he passed Steve Anderson, the state budget director.

"We're going to make it work," Anderson said to O'Neal. Making it work would be a lot more work than anticipated in the governor's proposal, given that the bill passed would cut revenue more than ten times the amount originally proposed through FY 2017.

O'Neal knew that meant lawmakers would have to find a way to reduce spending, but future cuts would never materialize. In the meantime, 2012 was an election year, and lawmakers would soon be heading home to campaign.

Table 7: Estimated Net Revenue Impact (millions)			
Fiscal Year	**Governor's Original Plan**	**Amended HB 2560**	**Senate Plan (law passed)**
FY 2013	$ (89.9)	$ (89.9)	$ (231.2)
FY 2014	$ (99.0)	$ (264.0)	$ (802.8)
FY 2015	$ (60.8)	$ (234.1)	$ (824.3)
FY 2016	$ (52.6)	$ (234.5)	$ (854.2)
FY 2017	$ (49.9)	$ (240.9)	$ (892.9)
Total	$ (352.2)	$ (1,063.4)	$ (3,605.4)
Source: Kansas Legislative Research Dept., Kansas Division of the Budget			

4

Adapting to Larger-Than-Expected
Tax Cuts

"The time to prepare the roof is when the sun is shining."
— John F. Kennedy

Brownback is often credited (or blamed) for what happened in the 2012 election, when conservatives replaced nine incumbents in the senate and maintained a healthy majority in the house. The governor, however, doesn't accept all of the blame or the credit.

"You've got to remember what really happened was that we had reapportionment," Brownback said.

Media wrote buckets about the 2012 tax reform, but tax reform occurred under the backdrop of redistricting. Efforts to reach a compromise between the senate and the house on reapportionment maps failed. Redrawing congressional maps and legislative districts fell to three federal judges.

"The court doesn't care who lives where. They're just drawing lines. [They] drew a bunch of conservatives and moderate candidates in the same senate districts," Brownback said.

The judges finished their efforts on June 7, 2012. The filing deadline to run for office was four days later, June 11. The new boundaries put several lawmakers into the same districts, while leaving some districts bereft of candidates.

According to the *Kansas City Star* (and conventional wisdom at the time), the maps favored moderate Republicans and Democrats.[104] They were dead wrong. "In 2012, you put a moderate up against a conservative in a Republican primary, the conservative generally won," Brownback said.

In district after district, moderate senators were pitted against more conservative house members for the senate seats.

"Tax relief sells," O'Neal said. "It still polls well. People would rather see reductions in spending than see their taxes raised."

Conservatives replaced nine incumbent senators. Republicans held a majority in both chambers before the 2012 election, but the senate was controlled by GOP moderates, who regularly worked with Democrats to block some of Brownback's initiatives. After the 2012 election, conservatives held a supermajority of twenty-seven in the forty-member senate. The number of conservatives in the house dipped slightly to about seventy-five of 125.[105] There weren't enough conservatives in the house to override a gubernatorial veto, but they shouldn't have needed to. They were on the same team as the governor.

"It was a political tsunami," O'Neal said. He didn't stand for re-election in 2012, so the former Speaker wouldn't be among the lawmakers attempting to align the 2012 tax plan with the state budget.

States That Spend Less, Tax Less—and Grow More

Restructuring the budget to accommodate an approximate 13 percent reduction in General Fund tax revenue certainly seemed impossible to many people but the solution was in understanding how states with lower tax burdens managed their finances. Every state provides the same basic basket of services (education, highways, social services, etc.), but some states do so at much lower costs and pass the savings on to citizens in the form of lower taxes. Kansas Policy Institute's analysis of all fifty states' spending per-resident published in a *Wall Street Journal* commentary was entitled "States that Spend Less, Tax Less—and Grow More."[106]

> Conventional thinking (at least within government) says that low state taxes are dependent upon having access to unusual revenue sources, but that's not it. A state could be awash in oil and gas severance taxes and still have a high tax burden if the government will not exercise restraint.
>
> The secret to having low taxes is controlling spending, and that's exactly what low-tax-burden states do. States with an income tax spent 42 percent more per resident in 2011 than the nine states without an income tax. States in the bottom 40 of the Tax Foundation's Business Tax Climate Index (which assesses business, personal, property and other taxes) spent 40 percent more per resident.

The data used in those analyses came from the National Association of State Budget Officers, excluding spending from federal sources and from debt issuance, and the disparity between high-tax and low-tax states has been consistent over the years. Analysis of 2015 actual spending from All Funds budgets with the same exclusions shows states that tax income spent 42 percent more per-resident; the ten highest-burden states spent 40 percent more and Kansas spent 27 percent more per-resident than the states without an income tax.[107]

The "grow more" portion of that *Wall Street Journal* commentary referenced the superior economic gains for the states with no income tax. Those nine states were Alaska, Florida, New Hampshire, Nevada, South Dakota, Tennessee, Texas, Washington, and Wyoming. The no-income-tax states had twice as much private sector job growth between 1998 and 2015 (37 percent vs. 18 percent), superior wage and salary disbursement (113 percent vs. 84 percent), and dramatically better GDP growth (126 percent vs. 93 percent). The states without an income tax gained population between 2000 and 2016 from domestic migration equal to 7 percent of their 2016 population and those net new residents came from states that tax income.

Table 8: States that Spend Less, Tax Less...and Grow More				
State Grouping	Private Sector 1998-2015			Domestic Migration 2000-16
	BEA Jobs	Wages & Salaries	GDP	
States with no income tax	37%	113%	126%	7%
States that tax income	18%	84%	93%	-2%
10 Lowest State & Local tax burden	33%	109%	127%	5%
10 Highest State & Local tax burden	20%	89%	97%	-6%
Source: Bureau of Economic Analysis, US Census. Domestic Migration reflects gains and losses as a percentage of 2016 population.				

Comparing the ten states with the lowest and highest combined state and local tax burdens also shows the low-burden states collectively have superior long-term growth in private sector jobs, wage distribution, and GDP, and unlike the states that tax income, they gain residents from domestic migration. That's not to say that low taxes alone are responsible for the superior economic performance of those states, but taxes are a variable cost, and the less people and employers must spend on taxes, the more they can spend elsewhere in the economy.

Governor Brownback took a lot of heat when he went on MSNBC's *Morning Joe* shortly after the 2012 legislation tax relief passed and said, "On taxes, you need to get your overall rates down, and you need to get your social manipulation out of it, in my estimation, to create growth. We'll see how it works. We'll have a real live experiment."[108] Tax-relief opponents objected loudly at the thought that funding for state services would be subjected to an "experiment" but supporters were also disturbed, partly because the "experiment" had arguably long since been concluded.

The group of states without an income tax and the ten states with the overall lowest state and local tax burdens consistently have superior economic performance as just explained, but that's just part of the conclusion to the "experiment" argument.

As explained in *An Inquiry into the Nature and Causes of the Wealth of States*, "Immediately prior to 1960, there were 19 states where earned income was not taxed and 31 states where it was. Between 1960 and [2014], 11 of those 19 states adopted an income tax and one state—Alaska—got rid of its income tax."[109] The eleven states that adopted an income tax were Maine, Rhode Island, Connecticut, New Jersey, Pennsylvania, West Virginia, Ohio, Indiana, Illinois, Michigan, and Nebraska.

The authors analyzed the impact of each state's new income tax on population, Gross State Product (GSP), and total state and local tax revenue relative to the other thirty-nine states as follows: "The percentage of each state's population to the total population of the 39 states in the five years prior to and including the year of adopting the income tax, the percentage of each state's population to the total population of the 39 states in 2012, the percentage of the total of the 39-state gross state (domestic) product for each of the 11 states in the five years preceding and including the year of adoption of the income tax, the percentage of the total of the 39-state GSP in 2012 for each of the 11 states, total state and local tax revenues as a share of the total of the 39 states' state and local taxes in the five years prior to adopting the income tax, and finally, each state's share of total 39-state state and local taxes in 2011."

Table 1.1

States That Added Income Taxes Versus States that Didn't

All 11 states that adopted an income tax after 1960 experienced declines in population, gross state product and state and local tax revenue.

State	First year of tax	Maximum Tax Rate*		Shares of 39 Remaining States								
				Population			Gross State Product			Total State and Local Tax Revenue		
		Initial	Current	5 Years Before	2012	% Chg	5 Years Before	2012	% Chg	5 Years Before	2011	% Chg
Conneccut	1991	1.50%	6.70%	1.81%	1.49%	(18)	2.39%	1.92%	(20)	2.35%	2.25%	(4)
New Jersey	1976	2.50%	8.97%	4.94%	3.68%	(26)	5.38%	4.25%	(21)	5.40%	5.25%	(3)
Ohio	1972	3.50%	5.93%	7.59%	4.79%	(37)	8.03%	4.27%	(47)	6.07%	4.46%	(27)
Rhode Island	1971	5.25%	5.99%	0.68%	0.44%	(36)	0.64%	0.43%	(33)	0.65%	0.50%	(22)
Pennsylvania	1971	2.30%	3.07%	8.51%	5.29%	(38)	8.49%	5.03%	(41)	7.66%	5.51%	(28)
Maine	1969	6.00%	7.95%	0.74%	0.55%	(25)	0.58%	0.45%	(23)	0.60%	0.60%	(0.2)
Illinois	1969	2.50%	5.00%	8.08%	5.34%	(34)	9.82%	5.82%	(41)	7.77%	5.89%	(24)
Nebraska	1968	2.60%	6.84%	1.10%	0.77%	(30)	1.03%	0.83%	(19)	0.93%	0.77%	(17)
Michigan	1967	2.00%	4.25%	6.33%	4.10%	(35)	7.86%	3.35%	(57)	6.62%	3.57%	(46)
Indiana[1]	1963	2.00%	3.40%	3.80%	2.71%	(29)	3.81%	2.36%	(38)	3.37%	2.29%	(32)
West Virginia[1]	1961	5.40%[2]	6.50%	1.54%	0.77%	(50)	1.19%	0.63%	(47)	1.09%	0.69%	(37)

* State tax rate only (does not include any addional local taxes).

[1] Due to data limitation, shares of personal income have been substuted for Indiana and West Virginia's shares of GSP.

[2] Statutory rate was 6.0% of U.S. tax liability applied to a top U.S. rate of 91%.

Source: U.S. Census Bureau, Bureau of Economic Analysis, Laffer Associates.

The results shown in Table 1.1 of the book (reprinted with permission) are stunning. In every single measurement for every single state, the states that adopted an income tax lost share of population, GSP, and state and local tax revenue relative to the other thirty-nine states. Think about that last one. They added a brand new source of revenue, and they still lost a share of state and local tax revenue!

With the knowledge that efficient, effective spending is the key to having low taxes, it became clear that Kansas needed only go from being morbidly inefficient to grossly inefficient in order to balance the budget at lower tax levels, as found in a dynamic analysis of the 2012 tax plan published by Kansas Policy Institute shortly following its passage.[110] A one-time General Fund spending adjustment of about 8.5

percent would have balanced the budget, leaving healthy ending balances and allowing spending to grow thereafter as revenue increased.

Even if General Fund spending had been reduced by 8.5 percent, it would still have been far ahead of long-term inflation. Spending of $6.098 billion in FY 2012 was almost $1.2 billion higher than if it had just been increased for inflation since 1995; a reduction of 8.5 percent would still have had spending $671 million ahead of long-term inflation.

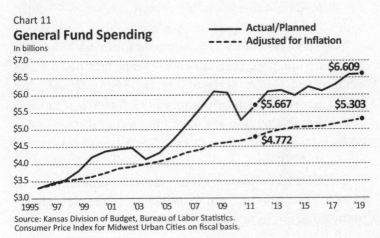

Chart 11
General Fund Spending
In billions

Source: Kansas Division of Budget, Bureau of Labor Statistics.
Consumer Price Index for Midwest Urban Cities on fiscal basis.

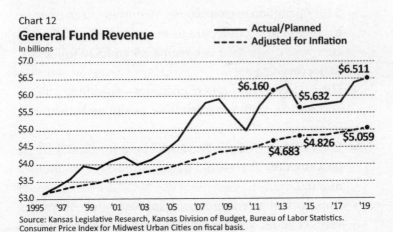

Chart 12
General Fund Revenue
In billions

Source: Kansas Legislative Research, Kansas Division of Budget, Bureau of Labor Statistics.
Consumer Price Index for Midwest Urban Cities on fiscal basis.

Media described spending cuts as being disastrous, devastating, and other harsh adjectives, but the data tells a different story. The year that the initial tax-relief bill was passed—FY 2012—the legislature increased General Fund spending by $432 million (7.6 percent) and set a new record. A tiny (0.6 percent) increase followed in FY 2013. Spending dropped a bit in FY 2014 then increased in FY 2015 by 4.2 percent and set another new record at $6.2 billion, followed by a gimmick-driven decline (deferred pension funding) in FY 2016. Yet another spending record was set in FY 2017, with a $181 million/3 percent increase.

State tax collections also continued to run well ahead of long-term inflation. Even after tax revenue dropped by $701 million in FY 2014, collections were still $806 million higher than if increased for inflation since 1995. By FY 2017, tax revenue was $897 million ahead of long-term inflation and if projections hold true, the new tax hikes will push collections almost $1.5 billion above long-term inflation by FY 2019.

State Budget Director Steve Anderson drafted a list of ideas to create government efficiencies, and he presented it to the governor in July 2012. It included:

- $20–60 million in payroll cuts. According to an internal memo from Anderson to Brownback the staffing cuts would also save between $7.5 and $20 million in overhead costs.
- Hiring freeze on certain positions—specifically IT, accounting, and administrative positions to begin immediately.
- Freeze State General Fund spending for capital improvements. That would have a saved $25.9 million in 2012.
- Cuts to higher education of approximately 10 percent, or about $74 million. (There was evidence that

universities were accumulating cash reserves and of multiple efficiency opportunities.)

- Initiate a contract review to find savings.
- Cut Kansas legislature budget by $2.7 million.
- Consolidate empty office space in Topeka and lease-back buildings.
- Examine replaceable asset schedule and extend life of replaceable assets like computers and machinery. The memo lists Kansas Highway Patrol vehicles as an example. Replace patrol cars after 60,000 miles instead of 50,000 miles.
- Require that those applying for or maintaining their professional licenses from the state, like teachers and lawyers, have filed Kansas taxes.
- Discontinue funding the Undermarket Salary Adjustments for a savings of $8.5 million in 2013.
- Outsource all accounting.

Most of the suggestions never saw the light of day in the Kansas legislature. Brownback marked the memo denoting a few ideas he thought were good and requested more information about others, and that was about the extent of it according to Anderson.

Brownback's Proposal

In his 2013 State of the State Address, Brownback declared his intent to shrink the size of government, but seconds later, he proposed a new spending initiative—a $12 million reading program that would help struggling elementary students learn to read. He assured lawmakers he wasn't interested in making cuts to schools or social programs. And he introduced the "march to zero," a so-called "ratchet" that would use revenue increases above specific targets to reduce marginal rates in future years.

"By making government more efficient and growing our economy, we can keep the sales tax flat at its current level and cut income taxes on our lower income working families to 1.9 percent and drop the top rate to 3.5 percent," the governor said. "This glide path to zero will not cut funding for schools, higher education, or essential safety net programs."[111]

The desire to shrink the size of government was sincere, but it didn't really materialize in the budget. The governor's Budget Report submitted in January 2013 proposed a 1.9 percent decline in FY 2014 from record-setting spending the year before and then a 1.1 percent increase in FY 2015.[112] Spending money is seen as the best insurance of getting re-elected, which is why rainy day fund proposals or tax and spending limitations (TELs) have been repeatedly rejected in Kansas. And when it appears that things are going well (as it did during the 2013 legislative session), finding the political will for spending cuts is even more difficult. As Mike O'Neal put it, "Politicians love to give out candy to everyone." In 2013, even the governor was in the mood to hand out treats and indemnify schools and social service programs from efficiency reviews.

Table 9: General Fund Spending (millions)	
Description	**Amount**
FY 2012 Actual	$6,098.1
FY 2013 Governor's Estimate	$6,198.4
FY 2014 Governor's Recommendation	$6,082.9
FY 2015 Governor's Recommendation	$6,149.6
Source: FY 2014 Governor's Budget Report, Schedule 2.2	

By the way, the proposal to spend $6.093 billion in FY 2014 was offered when the official forecast for General Fund revenue was only $5.464 billion.[113]

Anderson presented the governor's formal budget plan to the Ways and Means Committee shortly after the State of the State. The plan included adding some of the pay-fors left on the cutting room floor when lawmakers adopted the 2012 tax reforms. The governor proposed keeping six-tenths of a sales tax that was scheduled to expire that summer, which would generate $262.3 million for FY 2014. He also proposed eliminating the mortgage deduction on state income tax to generate $162.5 million.[114]

The governor also made a surprise announcement to eliminate the real estate tax deduction after the State of the State speech. While not included in the governor's Budget Report, the *Kansas City Star* reported that the plan "would affect roughly 372,000 Kansans who deduct their property taxes on their income taxes. The deduction saves the average taxpayer $125 a year. The home mortgage deduction trims an average $300 off income tax payments. In turn, the state would reap an added $68 million by dumping the property tax deduction."[115]

Lawmakers expressed concerns about those proposals almost immediately.

Republican Sen. Jim Denning told the *Kansas City Star* that those moves could be politically dangerous.

"It's going to be an uphill battle," Denning said.[116]

Despite the adoption of legislation in 2012 with a negative fiscal note of more than $800 million for FY 2014 and a legislature friendly to the governor, there wasn't much of an appetite for sweeping budget changes, according to Anderson. The former budget director says instead, the focus in the governor's inner circle moved to preparing for the 2014 gubernatorial election and Brownback's re-election efforts.

Sales Tax Fight

Lawmakers eventually passed legislation that included the "march to zero" income tax language, and itemized deductions received a retroactive "haircut" starting in 2013. The "haircut" eliminated itemized deductions for gambling losses, for example. The final bill also trimmed the standard deduction. For married couples, the standard deduction decreased from $9,000 to $7,500 and for head of household, the standard deduction dipped from $9,000 to $5,500. Lawmakers also restored a sales tax rebate program that they had ditched in 2012, however, the new legislation didn't allow refunds.

Legislators fought to the bitter end about whether to allow a sales tax to roll from 6.3 percent to 5.7 percent or keep some of the sale tax in order to assist in the march to zero. The sales tax rate, adopted in 2010, was set to sunset at the end of 2013.

Former Democratic Governor Mark Parkinson "had the gall" to request a 1-cent sales tax in his 2010 State of the State Address, as then Speaker of the House Mike O'Neal recalled. Parkinson was a former Republican who became a Democrat in order to serve as Governor Kathleen Sebelius's lieutenant. He became Kansas's governor when Sebelius was confirmed as the secretary of US Health and Human Services in the Obama administration.

"We are way beyond the point of cutting waste," Parkinson said in his 2010 address. "We face another budget hole of almost $400 million . . . We must raise our sales tax by one cent for a temporary period of 36 months. A temporary increase of just one cent allows us to fund our programs at the minimum acceptable levels while we work our way out of this recession. I am then proposing that after the third year the tax retreat, leaving just two-tenths of a cent in place that would be available to craft a moderate, but necessary, highway program."[117]

Republicans called it a non-starter at the time.

"Sales taxes harm the poorest in our society," Republican Rep. Arlen Siegfreid told the *Kansas City Star*.[118] "We're still in a recession. Now is the time to hold back on spending and wait this thing out."

Democrats expressed similar concerns.

"I'm not enthusiastic about it," Democratic Sen. Laura Kelly said. "I'm hoping we can find other ways to fill the hole."[119]

A bipartisan coalition eventually cracked and gave Parkinson the sales tax increase he sought. As O'Neal years later said, "Never underestimate the power of the governor."

Though most of Parkinson's sales tax increase was set to expire in 2013, Governor Brownback recommended maintaining it to stabilize projected dips in income tax revenue.

Brownback said he was eyeing the sales tax, because he hoped to move the tax load from production to the consumption side of the equation. It was a tough sell in the legislature, and media and progressive think tanks piled on. National Public Radio called the proposal to retain the existing sales tax rate "radical for a conservative Republican."[120] The Institute on Taxation and Economic Policy warned that replacing with sales tax just 50 percent of the state revenue lost from the 2012 income tax cuts would "wallop those with lower incomes."

Democrats said increasing sales taxes put additional tax burden on the poor, who spend a larger percentage of their budgets on sales taxes.

"It kind of eliminates a large group of Kansans out of that pursuit of happiness," Democratic Sen. Oletha Faust-Goudeau said. "They will still struggle. They'll pay the highest taxes. They are already working jobs with no benefits or very little benefits."[121]

Republican Rep. Tom Sloan said the governor's proposal was toppling Kansas's three-legged revenue stool comprised of taxes on income, sales, and property.

"So what we are doing is now saying we are going to have a two-legged stool, property taxes and sales taxes. I really don't know that that's a good way to fund the essential services that Kansans want—education, social safety net programs, public safety, and then investing in our future, whether that is preserving our state water supplies, or maintaining a viable highway system," Sloan said.[122]

When the senate Assessment and Taxation Committee considered Brownback's budget and tax proposal in February, debate lasted less than ten minutes.[123] The senate agreed to forward the legislation with few changes. Committee members agreed to maintain the higher sales tax rate of 6.3 percent, though they scrapped Brownback's recommendation to eliminate an income tax deduction for property taxes.

The full senate debated for five hours on the proposal, considering eleven amendments. Amendments to sunset the sales tax failed. Those that passed included one that gradually reduced most itemized deductions instead of eliminating them in one fell swoop. Another amendment fully eliminated gambling loss deductions. The final product passed the senate 25–14.

The house, however, dug in its heels on the sales tax increase. In early April, the house refused, 120–0, to concur with a conference committee report that included maintaining the 6.3 percent sales tax rate.

On May 30, the house rejected, 94–18, another compromise proposal that would have kept the sales tax at 6.3 percent and reduced grocery sales tax to 4.9 percent.[124] That was day ninety-seven of a ninety-day legislative session which house and senate leadership suggested at the start would last only eighty days.[125]

It was a legislative stalemate with the governor and senate on one side and the house on the other. By mid-May, the chambers had traded tax plans eight times. That number would eventually grow to eleven.[126] By the end of the month with the session in overtime, the stalemate continued.

The *Kansas City Star* opined on the final day of May: "The Kansas legislature should have convened in January with a clear mission: Find a way to maintain state services despite a gaping budget hole dug by reckless income tax cuts adopted in 2012. But almost five months later, lawmakers still haven't settled on an answer."[127]

The stalemate ended shortly after midnight on a Sunday morning, June 2. House Speaker Ray Merrick greased the wheels.

"If you're looking for the perfect solution, it's not going to be here," Merrick told Republicans in a Saturday morning caucus meeting.[128]

The compromise allowed a small portion of the sales tax to roll back to 6.15 percent, rather than the once-promised 5.7 percent. It also restored a food sales tax rebate program and cut itemized deductions for income taxes. All told, the package comprised in the Conference Committee Report for House Bill 2059 (HB 2059 CCR) was projected to raise $777.1 million in new revenue over the next five years. Democrats called it the largest tax increase in Kansas history.[129]

"This is a $777 million tax increase on working Kansas families, and this plan guarantees that your boss will stop paying taxes while your taxes go up," Kansas Democratic Party spokesman Dakota Loomis told the *Kansas City Star*.[130]

While retention of the higher sales tax was vocally opposed by many Democrats and moderate Republicans as a regressive tax increase on low- and middle-income families, many of them would eventually vote to raise income taxes on those same citizens in the 2017 legislative session and also retained the sales tax increase passed in 2015 (which they also denounced at the time). That many legislators would so easily abandon their principles once they regained majority control underscores one of the dirty secrets of the Kansas tax-relief effort—opposition to tax cuts had little if anything to do with policy; it was driven by a struggle for political power.

Consider Representative Sloan's defense of the three-legged revenue stool. If the concern was truly about the ability to fund essential services, legislators would embrace reducing or eliminating reliance on income taxes. Income tax receipts (individual, corporate, and financial institutions combined) plummeted 21 percent in Kansas between 2008 and 2010 due to the recession, but retail sales tax receipts only dipped by 3 percent over the same two years. Consumption taxes provide a much more predictable revenue stream regardless of economic conditions, whereas income tax spikes during boom years inevitably lead to higher spending, and that exacerbates the budgetary challenges in slow times. Legislators' preference for income taxes is more about social engineering (encouraging certain behavior like home ownership) and income redistribution.

Media and other tax-relief opponents would hound the Brownback administration in the coming years for not meeting its economic growth predictions relative to tax relief, but the passage of HB 2059 CCR—and more tax increases to come in the 2015 legislative session—marked another dirty secret. The original tax plan was never fully implemented, but those facts never stopped opponents from telling the story that suited their political goals.

The legislation passed in 2012 (Senate Substitute for HB 2117) was estimated to reduce taxes by $4.539 billion through FY 2018, but the tax hikes imposed in 2013 and 2015 would reduce relief to $2.428 billion, or just 53 percent of the original tax cut.

The impact of partially reversing course on the 2012 legislation went far beyond people having to pay higher taxes. Two tax increases and a steady demand from media and other tax-relief critics for full repeal of the original plan gradually created a great deal of uncertainty that had an incalculable but palpable impact, especially among the business community. The 38 percent reduction in expected tax savings for FY 2014 (from $802.8 million to $494.9 million) minimized the expected economic gains from individuals spending some of their tax savings on goods and services, which unfortunately coincided with downturns in two important sectors of the Kansas economy—the oil and gas industry and agriculture.

Fiscal Year	S Sub HB 2117 Passed 2012	HB 2059 CCR Passed 2013	S Sub HB 2109, H Sub SB 270, HB 2142 Passed 2015	Net Impact on Tax Revenue
FY 2013	$ (231.2)			$ (231.2)
FY 2014	$ (802.8)	$ 307.9		$ (494.9)
FY 2015	$ (824.3)	$ 217.1		$ (607.2)
FY 2016	$ (854.2)	$ 152.6	$ 384.4	$ (317.2)
FY 2017	$ (892.9)	$ 104.1	$ 404.8	$ (384.0)
FY 2018	$ (933.7)	$ (4.6)	$ 545.2	$ (393.1)
Total	$ (4,539.1)	$ 777.1	$ 1,334.4	$ (2,427.6)

Table 10: Net Impact of All Tax Changes (millions)

Source: Kansas Dept. of Revenue as provided by Kansas Legislative Research; rounding may affect totals.

2014 Legislative Session

With a two-year budget in place after the 2013 session and a looming election less than ten months away, fiscal issues took a back seat during the early part of the session. Governor Brownback kicked off the session with a State of the State advocating for new spending in the form of subsidies for low-income housing in rural Kansas and all-day kindergarten. At the time, the state only provided funding for half day, though some districts funded all-day programs through user fees, local funds, and other revenue sources. (That proposal didn't see the light of day in 2014, but lawmakers did increase school funding during the 2014 session.)

"Thanks to the growing economy and the work of this legislature, it is affordable," Brownback said in his address.[131]

Until the end of March, it appeared like the Kansas economy was humming. In January, state revenues exceeded expectations by $16.8 million. Corporate income tax receipts were 16 percent higher than anticipated, and despite the 2012 tax cuts, individual tax receipts brought in $4.5 million more than expected. Sales tax receipts were down, by 2.6 percent, or about $5 million less than expected.

"Corporate, income, individual, and use tax receipts point to an economy where businesses are growing, purchasing equipment, and creating jobs at a healthy rate," Revenue Secretary Nick Jordan said in a press release[132] at the end of January.

In February 2014, revenue beat projections by more than $100 million.[133] When revenues exceeded estimates by $130 million in March, the Kansas Department of Revenue Secretary Nick Jordan announced that the "Kansas economic engine is running."[134]

The next month, however, Kansas revenues hit the skids, missing projections by nearly $100 million. State officials pinned the blame, accurately, on federal changes in capital gains and a severe decline in agricultural and aircraft exports.[135]

"This is the slowest growth recorded since the last quarter of 2012 and has affected Kansas along with much of the nation," a KDOR monthly revenue press release stated. "While some economists expected this slowdown in GDP due to weather-related issues, the numbers released today indicate that other factors such as weakness in export, perhaps reflecting weak global economic activity, also played a substantial role in the slowdown during the first quarter of 2014."[136]

By May, revenues were down more than 47 percent year over year, thanks to the capital gains "fiscal cliff" and plummeting commodity prices as explained in Chapter 2. Kansas would consistently fail to meet revenue estimated until the revenue estimating process was partially revamped in 2016.

Missing Revenue Estimates

The emphasis in the 2014 legislative session shifted from policy changes to dealing with tax revenues coming in well below official estimates. Initially, tax collections were above consensus revenue estimates and Shawn Sullivan, the current Kansas budget director, believes that may have contributed to a false sense of security in 2013. Revenue estimators also weren't reading the tea leaves accurately.

"We're watching the economy the first year of the tax cut, and we had a record revenue year for the state of Kansas," Brownback said. "So the economy's performing well. And it looks like this is going to work, and it was."

A change in the federal capital gains tax, however, made it appear that revenues were running ahead of estimates, but with extra capital gains tax pulled forward to tax year 2013, a huge hole would be created in the 2014 tax year, and not just for Kansas. Effective January 1, 2013, the maximum rate on capital gains went from 15 percent to 23.8 percent; the capital gains rate itself increased to 20 percent and Obamacare simultaneously implemented a new 3.8 percent surcharge for incomes above $200,000 Single and $250,000 Married. The higher rate prompted capital gains to be pulled forward to 2012 and taxed at the lower rate and delivered unexpected windfalls to most states in 2013 when the taxes came due.

The national impact of this "fiscal cliff" effect was substantial, as described in a Rockefeller Institute of Government report. "The strong 19.4 percent income tax growth in April–June 2013 was the start of the federal 'fiscal cliff' cycle . . . as taxpayers accelerated income into 2012. It was followed by a 7.2 percent decline in personal income tax collections for the April–June 2014 quarter, which was the near mirror-image effect of the federal fiscal cliff."[137]

Figure 1 below from the Rockefeller Institute report shows a nearly 40 percent spike in final payments made in the second quarter of 2013 compared to the prior year, followed by more than a 20 percent decline in 2014.

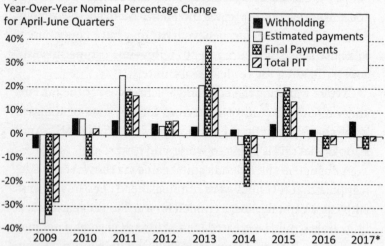

Figure 1

April-June Income Tax Collections are Volatile

Year-Over-Year Nominal Percentage Change
for April-June Quarters

Legend:
- ■ Withholding
- □ Estimated payments
- ▨ Final Payments
- ▧ Total PIT

*2017 uses growth rates for April and May combined as an estimate for the quarter.
Individual state data, analysis by the Rockefeller Institute
Source: "Shortfalls on States' April Tax Returns: Trump Effect, Weak Economy, or Both?"
Rockefeller Institute of Government, July 2017. Reprinted with authors' permission.

The Urban–Brookings Tax Policy Center's Howard Gleckman dismissed the fiscal cliff effect in Kansas without a shred of documentation, declaring, "A big chunk of that revenue decline likely comes from individuals redefining themselves as pass-through businesses. Last month alone the state's individual tax payments fell by one-third from June 2013."[138]

Gleckman added, "Keep in mind that these are actual year-over-year declines in revenues, not shortfalls in projected revenue. And they came at a time when the national economy was recovering (albeit slowly) and most other states were enjoying strong pickups in tax collections. Brownback and his defenders have blamed their revenue shortfall on the federal government (natch). They say that the fiscal cliff deal in late 2012 drove investors to accelerate capital gains realizations to beat a tax hike on investment income. It certainly did that, but given that gains are less than 10 percent of individual income, blaming the state's dramatic decline in revenue on capital gains timing is pretty lame. Besides, while Kansas individual income tax revenues bumped up a bit in [FY] 2013 over [FY] 2012 (as the fiscal cliff theory would suggest), the increase was only about $23 million."[139]

Sadly, jumping to conclusions of that nature was more the rule than the exception, and to use Mr. Gleckman's turn of phrase, it was pretty lame of professional journalists and researchers to make unfounded declarations. For starters, Gleckman ignored that Kansas cut income taxes for FY 2013 and collections were expected to decline by $231 million, but instead, collections increased by $23 million; the fact that collections actually *increased* over FY 2012 indicates something unanticipated took place and had more than a $23 million impact.

Table 11: Kansas Capital Gains by Adjusted Gross Income (millions)								
AGI Category	**2010**		**2011**		**2012**		**2013**	
Less than $1	$	61.7	$	71.0	$	75.9	$	82.8
$1 to $25k	$	(2.1)	$	12.5	$	26.1	$	49.9
$25k to $50k	$	35.4	$	49.8	$	56.3	$	88.3
$50k to $75k	$	62.5	$	70.6	$	96.9	$	126.9
$75k to $100k	$	77.2	$	84.8	$	109.7	$	148.1
$100k to $200k	$	255.4	$	269.7	$	356.9	$	464.2
$200k to $500k	$	327.7	$	354.7	$	528.0	$	515.1
$500k to $1 million	$	246.8	$	264.9	$	415.5	$	330.3
Over $1 million	$	1,962.8	$	1,633.0	$	2,485.7	$	1,546.6
All returns	$	3,027.3	$	2,811.1	$	4,151.1	$	3,352.2
Source: Internal Revenue Service; SOI Tax Stats accessed July 14, 2017								

Internal Revenue Service data in Table 11 shows a 48 percent spike in reported capital gains for the 2012 tax year, followed by a 19 percent decline the next year. Actual capitals gains tax collections cannot be calculated from this data alone since it's related to Adjusted Gross Income rather than Taxable Income, but it clearly was a major factor and exacerbated a persistent problem with official revenue estimates.

Kansas did have an unfortunate string of missing revenue estimates post-tax relief and some pundits almost took perverse joy in writing about the misses as proof that taxes should not have been reduced. Typically, however, media and other critics didn't bother to see if missing estimates was a new phenomenon or another long-standing tradition. Kansas Policy Institute did the research and discovered not only were revenue estimates routinely missed, the magnitude of the misses in some cases was far greater before tax relief.

The Kansas Consensus Revenue Estimating (CRE) group prepares General Fund revenue estimates in April and November of each year. The group is composed of representatives from the Division of the Budget (DOB), Kansas Department of Revenue (KDOR), Kansas Legislative Research Department (KLRD), and one consulting economist each from the University of Kansas, Kansas State University, and Wichita State University. The original revenue estimate for a fiscal year is prepared twenty months in advance and then revised each subsequent April and November; for example, the original FY 2014 estimate was prepared in November 2012 and then revised in April and November of 2013 and again in April 2014.

Table 12 reflects the percentage difference between the estimate for combined individual and corporate income tax collections and the actual amount collected for the year at each of those intervals. Variances are measured in pure percentage difference, with no distinction between positive and negative variances.

Table 12: Income Tax Estimate Variance Last 15 Years			
Relative to End of Fiscal Year	11-Yr Avg 2002-12	4-Yr Avg. 2013-16	15-Yr Avg Variance
20 months away	13.4%	4.8%	12.0%
15 months away	10.8%	5.8%	10.1%
8 months away	6.0%	6.3%	6.4%
3 months away	3.3%	4.9%	3.9%
Source: Legislative Research Division; Individual and Corporate income tax combined			

The first and second revenue estimates (twenty months and fifteen months away) were much more volatile in the eleven years preceding tax cuts, with an average miss of 13.4 percentage points on the original estimate compared to 4.8 percentage points in the first four years following tax cuts. A 10.8 percentage point variance occurred with the second estimate at fifteen months away from the end of the fiscal year, but the variance dropped to 5.8 percentage points following tax cuts. The third estimate at eight months away was nearly identical before and after tax cuts. The final estimate, just three months away from the end of the fiscal year, was more volatile after tax cuts, although most of that variance resulted from the "fiscal cliff" effect of capital gains taxes being pulled into FY 2013 and then plummeting in FY 2014.

Table 13: Income Tax Estimate Variance Last 15 Years		
Relative to End of Fiscal Year	Variance to Final	
	Percentage	$ (millions)
20 months away	12.0%	$305.7
15 months away	10.1%	$257.2
8 months away	6.4%	$161.7
3 months away	3.9%	$98.6
Source: Legislative Research Division; Individual and Corporate income tax combined		

Table 13 puts the variances into budgetary context using the fifteen-year average variance. The first two revenue estimates have significant bearing on legislators' future spending decisions as those estimates are used to formulate the next spending plan; the last two estimates occur within the fiscal year and are more about short-term decisions to balance the existing budget. Here we find that even the smallest variance of $98.6 million is material to state spending, which over that period averaged $5.47 billion. Estimates that are higher than actual revenue will squeeze reserves (if they exist) or cause last-minute spending adjustments, whereas year-end estimates that are significantly lower than actual revenue increase reserves—and often lead to demands for increased spending that then reset the base for subsequent years. Some states have mechanisms in place to direct excess revenue to rainy day funds or emergency funds that can only be tapped in specific circumstances, but not Kansas.

Many factors contributed to revenue estimates being persistently off target, including the process by which estimates were produced, insufficient information, and the expertise of those preparing revenue estimates. The CRE group consistently overestimated key economic indicators and thereby overestimated tax receipts. Table 14 compares GDP and Personal Income growth assumptions from the November 2013 revenue estimate with actual results from the Bureau of Economic Analysis for calendar years 2013 through 2015.[140] Estimated growth rates for GDP were far above actual growth each year; 44 percent, 31 percent, and 59 percent, respectively. Kansas did outperform the Personal Income estimate for calendar year 2013, but the estimate was 133 percent too high for 2014 and 120 percent too high for 2015.

Table 14: Growth Assumptions for Revenue Estimates			
Economic Indicator	**CY 2013**	**CY 2014**	**CY 2015**
Kansas GDP			
Assumed	2.6%	3.8%	4.6%
Actual	1.8%	2.9%	2.9%
KS Personal Income			
Assumed	2.0%	3.5%	4.4%
Actual	2.6%	1.5%	2.0%
Source: KLRD Nov. 2013 Consensus Revenue Estimate; BEA.			

Governor Brownback convened a working group in 2016 to examine the state's consensus revenue estimates, which produced these recommendations, to improve the process:[141]

1. Provide more timely, diverse, and accurate information during the economic outlook meeting and revenue forecasting meeting.
2. Invest in new economic and revenue modeling software.
3. Utilize statistical methods to develop a base projection for the major tax sources rather than a trend analysis.
4. Continue to restructure the Department of Revenue to build expertise and capacity within the Office of Research and Analysis.
5. Separate capital gains from the individual income tax forecast and estimate it separately. Approximately 80 percent of individual income tax receipts are payroll withholding taxes and much of the remaining is capital gains and is a volatile revenue source.
6. Change the composition of the CRE Group; contract with an independent economist for the economic outlook and revenue forecasting instead of using university economists.

7. Build greater transparency into the CRE process.
8. Pass legislation authorizing the mid-April estimate to be moved to May 1.

Despite long-standing issues with revenue estimate accuracy, Kansas legislators declined to adopt the simple recommendation to push the mid-April estimate back to May 1 so that all of April's critical collections could be taken into consideration. A hearing on HB 2133, a proposal to move the estimate to May 1, was held on February 8, 2017, in the house Appropriations Committee. Supporting testimony was provided by the state budget director, the secretary of Revenue, Kansas Chamber of Commerce, and Kansas Policy Institute. But even with no official opponents, the committee chairman decided not to "work" the bill in committee so no discussion or vote was taken.

No official explanation for not taking a vote was provided (even after one was requested), but it was simply raw politics. Amending the revenue estimating process would have acknowledged that something other than a change in tax policy was responsible for some of the revenue misses, and tax-relief opponents weren't about to let extenuating facts get in the way of their desire to hike taxes. And the mere fact that Governor Brownback's administration was suggesting the change was sufficient reason for some legislators to reject it, as animosity toward the governor obliterated any policy considerations—especially so for many of the newly elected legislators.

There was some concern that delaying the estimate a bit would leave less time to finalize the budget, but the legislature is in recess most of the time between mid-April and May 1 so there were multiple options to resolve that issue. As was almost always the case, even this minor tax issue was driven by political motivations at the expense of common-sense policy.

State Budget Director Shawn Sullivan was frustrated by the lack of political will to improve the revenue estimating process. "I think the revenue estimating process should be changed. We made as many changes as we could make in-house with computer simulations and sophistication. I want to follow the Working Group's recommendations and rely more on an independent economist. And when I bring that up continually to legislative leadership, they acknowledge the need to do that."

Leadership may have acknowledged the need for change, but they held firm to the status quo. Asked why legislative leadership wouldn't support his request or the recommendation of the CRE Working Group, Sullivan said, "They listened to KLRD, which didn't support change. The excuse I get is, well, it's been this way for forty-two years, and it's been accurate most of that time. Why would we change it now?" As shown above, revenue estimates have *not* been accurate most of the time, but leadership resists change because KLRD has the ability to guide legislators in the direction of policy preferred by an entrenched bureaucracy—and a perturbed bureaucracy can wreak havoc for legislators.

A Slow Bleed

Had anyone suspected the revenue hole was as deep as it eventually became—by the time the 2017 legislature met, it faced a projected $1 billion budget gap through 2019— lawmakers in 2014, 2015, and 2016 may have had more motivation to avoid increasing spending and consider making budget cuts.

That, Budget Director Sullivan said, goes back to the challenges state officials faced in their revenue estimating process.

"If we would have accurately predicted that at the time, then you would've had to do school cuts," Sullivan said.

Pending school financing lawsuits, a campaign season heating up, and imprecise revenue estimates limited the political will to make cuts, especially since it appeared deep cuts might not be necessary. Lawmakers tweaked tax policy in 2014, restoring a few tax credits that were eliminated in the 2012 tax reform, added $129 million in new funding for schools and courts, and called it a day. The 2014 legislative session marked the shortest one in more than forty years. Lawmakers were out of Topeka in mid-May, but they left knowing there would be budget challenges in the next year.

"If revenues don't grow like we think they will, we're going to have some difficult decisions. Next year's going to be challenging unless we have a tremendous increase," Republican Marvin Kleeb told the *Kansas City Star*.[142]

5

Still Kicking the Can
Down the Road

"The first lesson of economics is scarcity; there is never enough of anything to fully satisfy all those who want it. The first lesson of politics is to disregard the first lesson of economics."

—Thomas Sowell

Moody's Investor Service downgraded Kansas's credit outlook in April 2014 and Standard & Poor's did so shortly thereafter, prompting tax-relief opponents to act as though it spelled disaster and that cutting taxes was solely to blame. House Democratic Minority Leader Paul Davis, who was running against Brownback for governor that year, said, "Sam Brownback's irresponsible policies are blowing a hole in the state's finances, putting our schools at risk of more cuts, and causing our economy to lag behind our neighbors."[143]

Kansas's rating from Moody's dipped from Aa1 to Aa2 in 2014, which was still considered "high quality and very low credit risk." Media began theorizing the credit ratings drop was caused by the 2012 tax cuts, though Moody's analysts said the downgrade was related to a $129 million spending increase in schools, underfunded pension plans, and the inability to match spending with revenue.

"You put all those things together, and there's quite a bit of stress on the budget," Moody's analyst Lisa Heller told the *Kansas City Star*[144] in a story headlined, "Moody's

Downgrades Kansas' Credit Rating, Citing Sluggish Economy and Risky Tax Plan." Except Moody's *didn't* say the tax plan was risky; the *Kansas City Star* just made it up to inject their editorial opinion into a news story. Moody's said, "The downgrade reflects Kansas' relatively sluggish recovery compared with its peers, the use of non-recurring measures to balance the budget, revenue reductions (resulting from tax cuts), which have not been fully offset by recurring spending cuts, and an underfunded retirement system for which the state is not making actuarially required contributions."[145]

The economic conditions cited by Moody's were eerily similar to those listed in their April 6, 2011, notice of moving the Kansas outlook from stable to negative, long before tax cuts had even been discussed: "Weak pension funded status, continued use of non-recurring measures to achieve operating budget balance, repeated suspension of spending lid [waiver of ending balance requirement] and reported Fiscal 2010 General Fund balance was negative for a second year."[146]

There would be future dips in credit ratings and outlook, but Kansas bonds, as its still-high ratings suggest, remained high quality, low risk, and investment grade. However, the narrative was set. About this time, the term "structural imbalance" became part of the lexicon. The terminology was used to describe Kansas's budget a few times in 2014. It wouldn't become a major campaign issue until 2016, however. From May 2014 through the 2017 legislative session, media would breathlessly report every dip in credit outlook as a referendum on Kansas's 2012 tax reform.

2014 Gubernatorial Campaign

Education and taxes were the top concerns of voters heading into the 2014 gubernatorial election. According to a KSN News poll, conducted in the summer of 2014, some 34

percent of likely voters told pollsters that education funding was their top issue and 32 percent named taxes as their
primary concern.

Incumbent Governor Brownback faced House Minority
Leader Paul Davis for Kansas's top executive role, and polls
suggested it would be a very tight race. The KSN News poll,
for example, gave Davis a 47 percent to 41 percent edge over
Brownback.[147] Heading into election night, the Real Clear
Politics average gave Davis a 6-point edge.

Davis campaigned on returning the state to normalcy.
A centerpiece of Davis's campaign was a list of more than
one hundred Republicans, including many current and former elected officials, who endorsed Davis over Brownback.
Some, including former Republican State Senator and Senate
Majority Leader Steve Morris, blamed Brownback for their
own electoral losses in 2012.

"We traditionally have had a model that Republicans
and Democrats have used to grow the economy," Davis told
Business Insider.[148] "I think a lot of voters are just saying right
now that Governor Brownback just doesn't understand how
we've done things in Kansas and how we've been successful.
And that's why we're seeing him in a lot of trouble." Of course,
as explained earlier in the book, "how things were done in
Kansas" had led to economic stagnation, negative domestic
migration, school funding lawsuits, excessive spending, and
higher taxes.

Despite the stark differences between Davis and
Brownback, the gubernatorial race wasn't getting top bill-
ing in the state. That slot was reserved for an unusual race
for one of Kansas's US Senate seats. The race pitted incumbent Republican Sen. Pat Roberts and an independent,
newcomer, candidate Greg Orman, in a razor-thin race that
would help determine the majority party in the US Senate.
Outside groups funneled more than $10.5 million into what
would become the costliest race in Kansas history.[149]

Roberts won, and the efforts may have helped Brownback over the line. Voters re-elected both men. Roberts won 53.3 percent to Orman's 42.5 percent.[150] Brownback won capturing 50 percent of the votes compared to Davis's 46.1 percent. The makeup of the Kansas House remained largely unchanged, and in hindsight, it appears Kansas voters hesitantly opted to continue the status quo.

2015 Tax and Spending Increases

Brownback's second term, which officially started in 2015, was off to a rocky start. Tax receipts in January 2015 fell $47.2 million below expectations. State officials attributed the dip in revenue to a weaker than anticipated Christmas shopping season and an unusually large batch of refund checks being mailed out in January.[151] That was on the heels of a $15.1 million shortfall in the previous month.[152]

Lawmakers faced an estimated $648 million budget shortfall for FY 2016 when they arrived in Topeka for the legislative session in 2015.[153]

During his 2015 State of the State Address, the governor acknowledged that recent data on state revenues and expenditures, "present a clear challenge that must be addressed."[154]

Most elements of Brownback's 2015 tax proposal would ultimately become law. He recommended continuing the march-to-zero income tax, but at a slower rate. Under his proposal, the lowest income tax bracket would receive a small rate reduction in 2016, and then the march would be frozen until state revenues picked back up.

To address projected shortfalls, Brownback proposed increasing the tax on cigarettes by $1.50 per pack and raising the state sales tax on liquor to 12 percent from 8 percent. He also recommended reducing by 50 percent the income tax deductions for property taxes and home mortgage interest in 2015, rather than in 2017.

Prior to the session's start, Brownback transferred cash

balances from other state funds and made a series of cuts to eliminate $280 million from the budget. His cuts included a 4 percent reduction to cabinet level agencies and legislative agencies, and a 9.5 percent reduction in KPERS pension payments. Brownback filled more than $200 million of the shortfall by transferring funds from a variety of sources including the Children's Initiatives Fund and the State Highway Fund.[155] Along with revenue enhancements and transfers from other funds, Brownback projected the state would have a cash surplus in two years.

It took 113 days for lawmakers to hash out budget and comprehensive tax deals and close out the 2015 session. The final product included freezing income tax rates at 2.7 percent and 4.6 percent through 2017, and then allowing the bottom marginal rate to drop from 2.7 percent to 2.6 percent in 2018. A "ratchet" would then be used to lower income tax rates beginning in 2021 if tax revenue increased each year by more than 2.5 percent. The cigarette tax was increased by 50 cents per pack, and the sales tax rate from 6.15 percent to 6.5 percent. The tax deal, which increased taxes by $384 million, passed by the bare minimum number of votes required.

Democrats called it the "largest tax increase in state history," which it was—until they and moderate Republicans would pass an even larger tax increase in 2017.

"[Brownback's] 'glide path to zero' is a complete failure and will result in a self-inflicted budget crisis for years to come," Senate Minority Leader Anthony Hensley said.[156]

Brownback called it the opposite.

"Look at the totality of the picture," Brownback told the *Wichita Eagle*.[157] "When you look at that, it is a tax cut."

Local media, and especially opinion writers, were having none of it. A slew of editorials and columns rebuffed the 2015 package and Brownback's claims that Kansans should look at the net gains in Kansas's tax policy over the last few years.

Here are just a few headlines from the *Kansas City Star* in three days following passage of the 2015 tax package:

- Monday Poll Results: Many Find Fault with the New Kansas Tax Structure
- Only in Sam Brownback's Land of Oz Is a $400 Million Tax Increase Not a Tax Increase
- As Gov. Sam Brownback Signs Kansas Budget, He Denies That It Counts As a Tax Increase
- TheChat: Gov. Sam Brownback Calls Revenue Deal Not a Tax Increase
- Johnson County Socked By New $37 Million Sales Tax Increase In Reckless Kansas Budget.

Similar headlines dominated most Kansas newspapers. What started as a steady trickle of negative headlines became a flood. The flood never really subsided, and it got worse as the 2016 session and election approached.

Politics being what it is, some legislators who objected to the 2015 tax hike being characterized as a net tax cut would disavow claims that the record-setting $3 billion/five-year 2017 tax plan was a tax increase—claiming instead that it was just a return to the old system.

Another Spending Record

Despite continued concerns about projected budget shortfalls, lawmakers passed a budget that increased spending year-over-year. The 2014 state general fund spent $5.9 billion. In 2015, lawmakers adopted a budget that spent $6.2 billion.

The state faced an estimated $648 million budget gap when Brownback took the podium for his 2015 State of the State Address. Brownback attributed the deficit to increased school spending since 2014.

"A majority of the projected shortfall we face is due to increase in K–12 spending since Fiscal Year 2014," Brownback told members of the Kansas legislature. "I want to repeat that. A majority of the projected shortfall we face is due to increases in K–12 spending."[158]

He lamented the rate of budgetary growth; rightfully so. Though Brownback wasn't able to cut spending during his term in office, he did slow the rate of budget growth. Under the seven governors who preceded Brownback, spending grew an average of 8 percent; during Brownback's two terms, spending growth averaged 1 percent.[159]

Tax receipts weren't keeping pace with spending growth. In the last twenty-five years, the average growth in tax receipts was 3.6 percent.[160] As Brownback put it in his 2015 State of the State speech, "Forty governors held office before the state General Fund expenditures reached $1 billion for the first time. The next four governors saw that number hit $6 billion. That government spending growth was not reflective of the trajectory of our population [or] the economy. It was government getting too big, too fast. The era of ever-expanding government is over, because it has to be."[161]

The legislature didn't see it that way. Neither did Brownback. The budget he proposed for Fiscal Years 2015 and 2016 didn't cut the total amount of spending; the budget the legislature adopted didn't either. The governor recommended spending $6.36 billion, an increase over 2014's $5.983 billion. Lawmakers adopted a budget that spent $6.32 million from the state General Fund.

A chunk of new spending would come in the form of additional education funding. That wasn't Brownback's proposal; it was the result of court action in the summer of 2016.

At Brownback's behest, the 2015 Kansas legislature eliminated its school finance formula. The goal, as Brownback stated in his 2015 State of the State Address, was a "time out in the school finance wars."[162] Brownback said the formula at the time was not designed to be understood and locked in "automatic, massive increases in spending unrelated to actual student populations or improved student achievement. A formula which calculates that we have added more than 100,000 new students to the public schools while the actual census has grown by a fraction of that number—an accounting scheme that claims cuts to per pupil spending even as budget increases dramatically outpace increases in student population."[163]

During the 2015 session, lawmakers took Brownback's recommendation. They adopted a block grant system for funding schools. Under the plan, no schools would receive cuts in state aid, neither would they be guaranteed funding increases. The block grant funding was to be a two-year school funding program to give lawmakers time to craft a new funding formula.

Within weeks of the block grant funding passing the legislature, the issue was before a three-judge district court panel. In an eighty-seven-page ruling, the panel insisted the state reinstate the old school finance formula the legislature had scrapped just weeks prior. In their opinion, justices said the law was essentially an operational spending freeze and deemed the block grant funding did not meet Kansas constitutional requirements for adequate and equitable funding.

The state appealed the ruling to the Kansas Supreme Court, while using block grant funding for the 2015 and 2016 school years. The Kansas Supreme Court issued its ruling on the appeal shortly after the end of the 2016 legislative session warning it would close schools if lawmakers didn't return to Topeka and make funding more equitable for the following year. With only a few weeks before schools were to start, lawmakers took seriously the threat of seven Kansas Supreme Court Justices closing the doors of schools in the state's 286 districts.

Lawmakers had more than one option for easing what the court deemed "inequities." One proposal would have cut school funding by about a half of a percent in an effort to equalize. However, lawmakers opted for a different solution during a special session on June 24, 2016. They added $38 million in new education spending by using money from a planned sale of state assets, and agreed to take money from the K–12 extraordinary needs fund if the assets didn't bring in enough cash, using some tobacco settlement money and shaving money from some of the wealthier districts' allotments to divvy up between poorer schools in the state.[164]

Lawmakers passed the quick, legislative fix in short order. They were weeks away from an August primary election, and Kansas law prohibits raising campaign money from some special interests while the legislature is in session. In the 2016 August primaries, several conservative incumbents would lose their seats to moderate Republicans.

2016 Legislative Session

Lawmakers commissioned an efficiency study in 2015, and in January 2016 consultants from Alvarez & Marsal presented 105 recommendations to save money and generate revenue[165] worth a little more than $2 billion over the course of five years. The state paid $2.6 million for the study, but lawmakers and lobbyists began shooting down proposed efficiencies from the day they were first presented.

Proposals to create efficiencies in school spending comprised savings of more than $600 million. They included creating a statewide health insurance plan for teachers and creating efficiencies through group procurements for things like computers. Legislation for those proposals stalled in committee the 2017 session, but opposition started before legislation was written. Alvarez & Marsal also recommended capping school operating cash reserves at 15 percent of current operating spending for each district and using excess reserves to reduce state aid to schools. That commonsense approach wouldn't have reduced funding available to schools because they could use their excess cash balances, most of which represented funds provided in prior years but not spent; it was estimated to save $193 million, but legislators lived in fear of the school lobby's ability to get them un-elected and found excuses to ignore the recommendation.

As early as January 2016, Democratic Sen. Laura Kelly said she didn't believe that creating a statewide health plan for schools would result in $123 million in savings, as the A&M study suggested. The executive director for the Kansas Organization of State Employees called the recommendation "short-sighted," because it would "erode paychecks and make the state an even less attractive place to work."[166]

Other recommendations included:

- $40 million in savings by fully utilizing Kansas Correctional Industry, which employs inmates to manufacture products purchased by state agencies;
- $170 million in savings by changing the way the state bids out, purchases, and administers insurance policies;
- $8.5 million in revenue generation by increasing sponsorships for rest stops, travel assist hotlines, and roadside sign logos;
- $3 million in savings by leasing or selling underutilized Kansas Department of Transportation equipment;
- $28 million in savings by consolidating nearby KDOT offices;
- $40 million in savings by consolidating some state technology services;
- $381 million in revenue generation by filling sixty-eight vacant revenue collection and auditor po-sitions and reorganizing audit and collections staff.

As of this writing, most of the high-dollar efficiency rec-ommendations sit in a desk somewhere because legislators couldn't muster the political will to implement them. Few efficiencies were implemented, though Shawn Sullivan, budget director, said the administration implemented many of the efficiencies that didn't require legislative approval.

Tales of an LLC Loophole

Though it would become a common refrain during the 2016 campaign for state offices, the term "LLC loophole" didn't really enter the common lexicon until early February of 2016. It was a term coined by Republicans. Lieutenant Governor Jeff Colyer used the term while defending the pass-through tax exemption at a Northeast Johnson County Conservatives meeting on February 3. A few days later, Sen. Jim Denning, then chair of the senate Ways and Means Committee, used the term speaking with a columnist for the *Kansas City Star*.[167]

"The governor rolled the dice on the most aggressive tax cut policy in history, and things just did not turn out the way he expected," Denning said.

Denning took that bet, too. He voted for the 2012 tax exemption when he was a member of the house. He would become one of the loudest advocates for eliminating the pass-through exemption in 2016. "We should have closed the loophole last year. We had the votes, but the governor threatened to veto any change to his signature business exemption tax policy. If we would have closed the loophole, we would have brought in an additional $200 million, and the governor would have been a hero," Denning said.

He told columnist Steve Rose that he was "fatigued from mopping up the mess" of having revenues that do not meet expenses.

Denning testified before the senate Ways and Means Committee in April 2016 on SB 508, which would revoke the income tax exemption on pass-through income. He told members that the loophole was never what the Kansas legislature intended and that it was implemented incorrectly by the Kansas Department of Revenue.

"It is not fair to wage earners who pay taxes to see their counterparts in LLCs have the income earned from their labor exempt from tax," his written testimony to the committee reads.[168] Sen. Jeff King, a Republican, submitted identical testimony. ("LLC" became the generic term often used to reference all of the pass-through entities.)

Legislators had been told that owners of pass-through businesses would still pay income taxes on the salary income they took themselves, but it wasn't understood that some pass-through entities weren't required to declare salary income for federal tax purposes.

Republican Sen. Greg Smith also offered testimony in support of eliminating the exemption, calling it "a mistake."

"The interpretation of holding all income harmless was a mistake—never the intent of the bill that I voted for," Smith's written testimony reads.[169]

After the session ended, Denning told the *Star* that business people who benefitted from the pass-through exemption were feeling like "freeloaders."

"Everybody should pay their fair share of taxes when businesses are profiting," he said.[170]

Fairness Wasn't Really the Issue

Exempting pass-through income from state income tax created a legitimate fairness issue that many legislators cited as a primary reason for wanting the exemption eliminated. They were loath to be reminded, however, that the original class to be exempted from state income tax was not partnerships, sole proprietors, Sub-S corporations, and LLCs, but state and local government pensioners. Retirees of state universities and the Board of Regents participating in their 403(b) plan are exempt from state income tax on withdrawals, whereas private sector Kansans are fully taxed on their pension and 401(k) withdrawals.

Retirees of other state agencies, school districts, and local governments participate in the Kansas Public Employees Retirement System (KPERS). They are taxed on their personal contributions to the pension program but are never taxed on the majority of their withdrawals, which come from employer contributions and earnings on all contributions. And legislators get an even better deal. In addition to preferential tax treatment, their pensions are based on having worked a full year and earned about $85,000 instead of what they are actually paid—less than $10,000 per year.

Other fairness issues that the legislature declined to address include:

- The legislature allows local governments to exempt chosen businesses from state and local sales tax with the use of STAR bonds and Industrial Revenue Bonds, which results in others being taxed more to make up the difference.
- The legislature provides sales tax exemptions to a wide array of business activities, services, retail purchases, and many non-profit organizations totaling more than $5 billion dollars annually.
- The State of Kansas's High Performance Incentive Program (HPIP) exempts businesses selected by government from sales tax and provides income tax credits. The Promoting Employment Across Kansas (PEAK) program allows businesses chosen by government to keep 95 percent of their eligible employees' state income tax withholding for up to ten years.

And despite their stated desire to make the tax system fairer, the 2017 legislature would create new tax credits for graduates of aerospace and aviation education programs and their employers.

Tax Avoidance

Another major justification for eliminating the income tax exemption on pass-through income was that the policy had led to massive tax avoidance.

The pass-through exemption for years was assailed by media and others as causing massive tax avoidance and resulting in much lower revenues than expected, which in turn caused deep budget shortfalls. To read most reports, one would think tax avoidance and related budget issues were an open-and-shut/absolutely proven matter—but it was all conjecture.

Tax return data from the Internal Revenue Service and the Kansas Department of Revenue refutes claims of significant tax avoidance. According to KDOR, "In 2011, when the tax policy was estimated, KDOR referred to federally held IRS data. The most recent dataset available at the time was for tax year 2009 and it had three categories of returns that would be considered as tied to a personal business; Business or Profession Net Income, Number of Farm Returns, and Partnership/S-Corp Net Income."[171] Those entities as well as income from rents and royalties are reflected on Schedules C, E, and F.

There were 191,991 Schedule C proprietors in 2009, which is very close to the number of entities used in legislative and media discussions, but including farm returns from Schedule F and other entities from Schedule E, Kansas actually had 329,511 total pass-through entities in 2009.[172] There were 333,590 pass-through entities in 2012 and the most recent data from 2014 shows 339,980 entities. The IRS data clearly shows the original estimate was inaccurate and should have been in the vicinity of 330,000.

Interestingly, state officials were aware of the error for an unknown period of time but didn't mention it; simply correcting the mistake early could have avoided much heartache and put media on notice. The Tax Foundation eventually published corrections of its tax avoidance claim and other errors on its website, but by the time it did so, the damage of the previous months and years was done.

Table 15: Pass-Through Entities on IRS Returns				
Tax Year	Schedule C Proprietors	Schedule F Farm Returns	Schedule E Partnership, S-corp, Rent, Royalties	Total Entities
2005	192,578	61,372	Not Reported until 2009	253,950
2006	194,753	61,566		256,319
2007	200,151	62,039		262,190
2008	192,622	60,339		252,961
2009	191,991	59,053	78,467	329,511
2010	193,323	59,053	79,115	331,491
2011	194,338	58,286	80,935	333,559
2012	194,330	57,270	81,990	333,590
2013	197,660	56,570	83,860	338,090
2014	199,250	55,850	84,880	339,980
Source: IRS Tax Stats				

Some C-corporations did convert to pass-through status, but it was not much different than the year prior to the exemption going into effect. According to the Kansas Department of Revenue, C-corp conversions for 2012 through 2014 shows just a slight increase in the rate of conversion to pass-through; it was 1.3 percent in 2012 (the year before the exemption was enacted) and the average for 2013 and 2014 was 1.7 percent.[173]

KDOR data on withholding payments[174] also refutes the notion that a large number of individuals convinced their employers to convert them from W-2 wage reporting to tax-exempt independent contractors. Calendar year withholding declined 14 percent in 2013, but that's less than the cut in marginal tax rates. The rate for the lowest bracket ($15,000 single; $30,000 married) declined by 14.3 percent and the tax on income above those levels declined by 21.6 percent and 24 percent, respectively. Further, any significant conversion would have been noticeable on the IRS Schedule C data, but that didn't occur.

Table 16: Marginal Rate Change				
Single	Married	2012 Rate	2013 Rate	Change
$0+	$0+	3.50%	3.00%	-14.3%
$15,000+	$30,000+	6.25%	4.90%	-21.6%
$30,000+	$60,000+	6.45%	4.90%	-24.0%
Source: Kansas Department of Revenue				

The notion of a "massive tax-avoidance scheme" is also refuted in the findings of a 2016 academic study. "The Impact of State Taxes on Pass-Through Businesses: Evidence from the 2012 Kansas Income Tax Reform" documented three main findings: "First, we find a small increase (2 percent) in the probability of reporting income from self-employment, though we fail to find similar increases for other types of pass-through businesses. Second, despite a small, statistically significant decrease in wages, we find no evidence that the amount of reported pass-through income was impacted. Finally, consistent with the observed increase in reports of having self-employment income, we find evidence suggesting that wage income may have been shifted to contract income in order to receive preferential tax treatment."[175]

Despite finding only a small increase (2 percent) in the *probability* of reporting from self-employment and no evidence that reported pass-through income was impacted by a small decrease in wages and that some wage income *may have* been shifted to contract income, the study's authors concluded that "the behavioral responses were overwhelmingly tax avoidance rather than real supply-side responses."

Art Hall, director of the Brandmeyer Center for Applied Economics at the University of Kansas School of Business, called their research efforts the gold standard. "But when they describe their results, it's pretty weak," Hall said in response to the study.[176] "Their magnitude of numbers are relatively small. They caveat themselves throughout the paper. They're admitting it's pretty weak." Regarding motivation for changing employment status, Hall said, "It's going to be hard to know why people did what they did, because the magnitudes are so small. They tried to test for that, but they still don't know."

Saving money on state income tax could be a motivation, but there are mitigating factors that could negate or even prevent a transition from wage earner to contract employee. Wage earners pay 7.65 percent in employment tax (up to a maximum of $127,200 for the 2017 tax year, after which the rate drops to 1.45 percent) for Social Security and Medicare, and their employer pays the same amount. The IRS considers self-employed individuals as both employer and employee for this purpose, so switching from wage earner to self-employed contract worker cost an effective 3.8 percent of earnings in employment tax to avoid paying a maximum 4.6 percent in income tax (the IRS allows a 50 percent deduction of the additional payroll tax cost). Switching to self-employment would also mean relinquishing all employer benefits such as health care and retirement and paying for them out of pocket; the cost would be a deductible business expense that reduces the self-employment payroll tax but there could be a net cost increase under some circumstances.

Employees would also have to convince their employers to relinquish a great deal of control over them to become a self-employed contract worker. Bill Pickert, managing partner of the Wichita Office of BKD, LLP, said, "There are very specific IRS rules that have to be applied to the individual facts and circumstances to make the determination of independent contractor versus employee. The rules are written in such a way as to make classification of a worker as an employee as the default answer and it would normally be difficult for an employee to meet the independent contractor standards, thus making conversion to a self-employed independent contractor to avoid Kansas income tax very difficult."

"Burn It Down" Mentality

SB 508 didn't make it out of the Ways and Means Committee so the full senate never voted on it, but the house did have an opportunity. Republican Rep. Mark Hutton used a parliamentary procedure to strip one bill and replace it with legislation to kill the pass-through exemption on the house floor (House Sub for SB 63). It was torpedoed after twenty minutes of debate in the Kansas House but not before providing another window into the "burn it down" mentality of some legislators. It had become apparent over the years that some legislators really had no interest in resolving the budget issue; prior to the 2017 legislative session there was no legislation introduced by Democrats or many Republicans to balance the budget with cost reductions and only one proposal in the 2016 legislative session (HB 2672) by Democrat Representatives Henry Helgerson and Ed Trimmer to increase taxes (eliminate the pass-through exemption). The desire for political power (de facto control of the house and senate by a coalition of Democrats and Republicans) and embarrassment of fiscal conservatives took precedent.

House Sub for SB 63 fell eighteen votes short of passing, with twenty-four voting "No" who had repeatedly said all business income should be taxed. A few who voted "No" said they didn't have enough time to review the bill, but that hardly passed the smell test; income that would be newly subject to taxation, the rates, and the amount raised annually were all very clear, and the concept is what they had been proposing for four years. Even the *Wichita Eagle* said Democrats and GOP moderates wimped out on the tax vote.

"Democratic and moderate GOP state lawmakers spent much of this legislative session complaining about the fairness of the state exemption for pass-through business income. They also noted how it was damaging the state's finances without significantly boosting the state's economy," an *Eagle* editorial reads. "Yet many of them voted last against a bill to revoke the exemption. Wimps."[177]

The editorial concluded, "Democrats may have balked at voting for the bill because they wanted to force the GOP to clean up its own mess—and suffer the political consequences. Many moderate Republicans likely feared that groups such as Americans for Prosperity would target them during this year's GOP primary, sending out postcards blasting them for voting to raise taxes. They may have made a political calculation that the bill might not clear the Kansas Senate, so it wasn't worth voting for it and, in doing so, placing a target on their backs. But if they are afraid to make tough votes and go on record for what they believe, why be a lawmaker? To their credit, several lawmakers did stand up, including Reps. Henry Helgerson, D-Eastborough, and Tom Sawyer, D-Wichita, who spoke passionately about the need to revoke the exemption. But too many other Democrats and GOP moderates acted like cowards."

Others who voted "No" said the bill didn't go far enough. Democratic Rep. Tom Burroughs explained his vote to the *Wichita Eagle*:[178] "It doesn't get to the root of the problem. It's a very small piece. If they were really serious about resolving the tax issue, they would have talked about all the tax policy." The other piece of the 2012 tax reform was income tax relief for all Kansans, but Burroughs stopped short of explaining that.

"Here we are late in the session once again, trying to do tax policy on the fly," Burroughs said. "While this is an important piece of the pie, this isn't everything that needs to be fixed."

Moderate Republicans also declined to vote to repeal the

pass-through exemption, which was projected to add $220 million to state coffers when fully implemented in 2018.

A moderate Republican, Rep. Barbara Bollier, called the vote a "gotcha." "It had nothing to do with doing the right thing. The right thing is to fix the problem. We need more than this," she said.[179] They didn't need more money, or any tax increase for that matter; they just wanted it. They also had a political motive. The 2016 election was mere months away, and the continued existence of the pass-through exemption could be used as campaign fodder. It would later be used as leverage for the largest tax increase in Kansas history during the 2017 session.

Lawmakers never would vote on the singular issue of revoking the pass-through exemption or capping it during the 2017 legislative session, and Democratic Sen. Laura Kelly revealed the reasoning.

"If we take that part out of the overall tax plan, we take all of our leverage out," she said.[180] "The real money in the tax cuts was not in that provision. It was in the reduction of the [income tax] brackets."

And that's what they would eventually get. The majority of the 2017 income tax increase—$1.8 billion of the $3.0 billion/five-year total—would be imposed on individuals.

6

2017 Legislative "Sea Change" Sinks Tax Cuts

"The way of the pioneer is always rough."

—Harvey S. Firestone

Pundits and critics called the 2016 Kansas legislative elections a repudiation of Gov. Sam Brownback's policies. "This is a sea change," Steve Kraske, a *Kansas City Star* reporter and public radio host, intoned on November 9, 2016, the day after the election.[181]

In the 2015–16 legislative session, there were ninety-seven Republicans in the Kansas House to twenty-eight Democrats. The Democrats gained twelve house seats in the 2016 election. More importantly, a similar number of Republican seats went from conservative to moderate.

"Whatever conservative Republicans have wanted the last five or six years they've been able to do, but that changes now. Between the new Democrats who've been elected and moderate Republicans who are moving on. They form a coalition now. There's enough votes there in the state house to block conservative initiatives. So it's a new day," said Kraske.

Kraske may feel conservatives did whatever they wanted in the past, but that wasn't necessarily so. Self-described fiscal conservatives say they believe in efficient government, yet some of them opposed substantive efforts to rein in wasteful spending. One also cannot view "Republican" and "fiscal conservative" as interchangeable descriptors, especially in Kansas. Republicans may have had a 97–28 majority in the 2015–16 legislative session, but then Speaker of the House Ray Merrick said, "It was never easy to get sixty-three votes on real conservative issues. It's a lot easier to spout conservative talking points during the election process than it is to make hard votes."

More critically, lawmakers moved away from the principles of economic freedom in 2017. Every year since 2012, Kansas Policy Institute has published the Kansas Freedom Index, ranking legislators based on their commitment to economic freedom, student-focused education, and federalism.[182] Positive points are awarded for votes in support of those principles, with negative scores reflecting votes in opposition. In order to compare scores across multiple sessions, raw scores are converted to percentages on a number line basis, with a score of zero equaling a freedom index of 50 percent—voting for and against freedom issues with the same regularity. A higher score means a lawmaker voted more often in favor of economic freedom.

Underscoring the point that party affiliation isn't an indicator of principles, KPI said, "Just as in years past, political party seemingly has nothing to do with votes on freedom-related issues. In fact, in both the House and Senate the highest and lowest scores are held by Republicans. This also isn't a product of outliers on either end. Indeed, the 12 lowest scores in the House and 14 lowest in the Senate are all Republicans. Across both chambers 47 Republicans were above 50 percent and 70 Republicans were below 50 percent; 50 percent effectively being "neutral" on issues of economic and educational freedom. Only one Democrat was above 50 percent."[183]

While Republicans boasted the highest and lowest scores in the Kansas House and the Kansas Senate, as a whole, both bodies scored significantly lower than in prior years.

House Republicans voted in favor of free markets and liberty 42 percent of the time in 2017. In 2016, they voted in favor of freedom 70 percent of the time. In the senate, Republicans voted in favor of freedom principles 39 percent of the time in 2017, compared to 68 percent in 2016.

Table 17: Kansas Freedom Index						
Categories	2012	2013	2014	2015	2016	2017
House						
Republican avg	67%	62%	63%	54%	70%	42%
# Repubs 75%+	35	14	18	3	41	10
# Repubs 25% or below	0	0	0	0	0	38
Democrat avg	21%	38%	30%	51%	26%	29%
# Dems 75%+	0	0	0	0	0	0
# Dems 25% or below	25	0	7	0	15	13
Senate						
Republican avg	51%	64%	64%	55%	68%	39%
# Repubs 75%+	3	5	6	1	6	5
# Repubs 25% or below	4	0	1	0	0	16
Democrat avg	21%	32%	28%	47%	33%	27%
# Dems 75%+	0	0	0	0	0	0
# Dems 25% or below	6	1	3	0	0	1

Leadership in both bodies also scored significantly lower on KPI's Freedom Index. House leadership scores dropped from 67 percent in 2016 to 29 percent in 2017. Senate leadership index scores also plummeted from 62 percent to 26 percent.

The dramatic shift wasn't readily apparent until the 2017 legislative season kicked into high gear, though signs were evident throughout the 2016 campaign. Self-proclaimed moderate Republicans campaigned heavily on eliminating the pass-through exemption, even though some of them voted *against* eliminating it in 2016 (as did several Democrats). A number of Republicans who voted for the LLC-tax incentive in 2012 also campaigned on eliminating the provision in 2016. Increasing school funding was perhaps the central issue of the 2016 campaign, but a few incumbents made the LLC-tax incentive a campaign centerpiece with varying results.

Sens. Mary Pilcher-Cook and Jim Denning

Johnson County was ground zero for candidates who voted for the 2012 tax reform, before they came out against it. A wealthy, suburban county within the Kansas City metropolitan area, Johnson County is often called the economic engine of Kansas. Its eastern edge is the Missouri border. Two Johnson County senate candidates offered a quick case study on the LLC-incentive as a campaign issue.

Sens. Mary Pilcher-Cook and Jim Denning are Johnson County Republicans. Both voted for the 2012 tax reform. Denning voted for the tax reform as a member of the Kansas House, while Pilcher-Cook cast a vote in favor of the tax cuts in the senate. By the 2016 election, both were running to retain their seats in the senate.

During the 2016 legislative session, Denning laid the groundwork for making the LLC-exemption the center of his campaign. Along with Republican Sens. Greg Smith and Jeff King, Denning sponsored legislation to roll back the LLC-tax incentive.

"We must close the LLC loophole. It grows bigger every year, costing Kansas at least $250 million annually," Denning said in a written statement issued in March of 2016. "It continues to make the budget unstable."

Attempts to repeal the pass-through exemption failed, but Denning would continue a drum beat of killing the exemption throughout his re-election campaign efforts in the summer and fall of 2016. Meanwhile, Pilcher-Cook campaigned as a fiscal conservative who would fight to retain tax cuts, including the pass-through exemption.

They campaigned in very similar districts on very different platforms. In Denning's district, 47 percent of voters are registered Republicans, and 23 percent are registered Democrats. In Pilcher-Cook's, 43 percent of voters are Republicans, and 25 percent are registered Democrats.

Though their districts are very similar, Denning enjoyed a slight numbers advantage on paper.

Denning also enjoyed an advantage in terms of his opponent. He faced Democrat Don McGuire. Pilcher-Cook faced Democrat Vicki Hiatt. McGuire raised $20,000 during his campaign to Denning's $160,000. Hiatt raised $60,000 to Pilcher-Cook's $100,000. Advantage: Denning.

The major difference between Denning and Pilcher-Cook's races was in how they campaigned. Both boasted similar voting records. They voted against the 2015 sales tax increase, supported block grant funding of schools, and opposed Medicaid expansion.

They campaigned differently on a few things, however. Pilcher-Cook voted against the education funding bill that came out of the 2016 special session; Denning voted for it.

Though Denning voted to implement the LLC-tax incentive in 2012, he campaigned as a vocal opponent of it in 2016. He campaigned heavily in favor of revoking the tax incentive. He campaigned as an anti-Brownback Republican. Pilcher-Cook campaigned in favor of maintaining the tax incentive and as a Brownback Republican.

Both Denning and Pilcher-Cook narrowly won re-election. Denning beat McGuire 52.7 percent to 47.2 percent. Pilcher-Cook defeated Hiatt 51.5 percent to 48.6 percent.

Denning's margin of victory was 1.2 percentage points higher than Pilcher-Cook's, and that was despite the fact Pilcher-Cook faced a better-funded opponent and much more engaged opposition. Working to overturn the tax cut wasn't necessarily an electoral winner, according to Jared Suhn with political consultant The Singularis Group. Referencing the Political Voting Index (PVI), which scores house districts based on how red or blue they are, Suhn said, "Senators Denning and Pilcher-Cook are in very similar districts, yet both won despite being on opposite sides of the pass-through issue. And being in more conservative districts didn't save incumbents who flipped and proposed repealing the LLC tax."

Phony Deficits

Based on PVI scores, it appears the 2016 Kansas electoral wave was an anti-incumbent one or a referendum on the state of school funding, rather than a repudiation of Brownback's tax policy. After all, Brownback's tax policy went into effect in 2013 and hadn't changed, yet the 2014 election saw Republicans gain seats. The LLC-exemption was but a sideshow.

When lawmakers arrived in Topeka for the 2017 legislative session, they faced a widely publicized but somewhat misleading $900 million gap between projected spending and revenues over the next two years. Media persisted in reporting that Kansas had a $900 million, two-year budget deficit throughout the 2017 legislative session despite knowing that the real number was considerably lower. The reported deficit included $192.6 million of statutory "transfers out," or revenue reductions that hadn't been approved in over a decade and another $6 million that hadn't been approved for two years. Collectively, these spending items overstated the budget shortfall by $205.6 million.

Table 18: Transfers Inflating the Budget Deficit (millions)						
Scheduled Transfers	**FY 2018**		**FY 2019**		**Total**	
Bioscience Initiatives	$	6.0	$	60.0	$	66.0
Local Ad Valorem Tax Relief	$	-	$	54.0	$	54.0
City County Revenue Sharing	$	-	$	72.6	$	72.6
State Water Plan	$	-	$	6.0	$	6.0
Transfers that won't occur	$	6.0	$	192.6	$	198.6
Regents Infrastructure Maint.			$	7.0	$	7.0
Totals	$	6.0	$	199.6	$	205.6
Source: Kansas Division of the Budget						

Each item listed in Table 18 is considered a "transfer" of revenue rather than appropriated amounts of spending because they were written into statute in that manner. Most spending is done through the appropriations process but statutory transfers are a slick way of avoiding the appropriations process so spending flies under the radar of citizens and even some legislators. The mechanism used in Kansas also understates actual tax collections because revenues are reported "net" of transfers out and refunds.

The Bioscience Authority no longer existed, but $66 million was still scheduled to be scraped off the top from tax revenue and sent to it. Local Ad Valorem Tax Relief (LAVTR) and City County Revenue Sharing (CCRS) were last funded in 2003; instead of removing the statutory appropriation, past legislatures simply amended the law to say "except this year." The transfer to the State Water Plan subsidized water usage for those who received free water (mostly farmers who irrigated) and hadn't been funded for the previous two years.

Chart 13
Cumulative Change in Property Tax

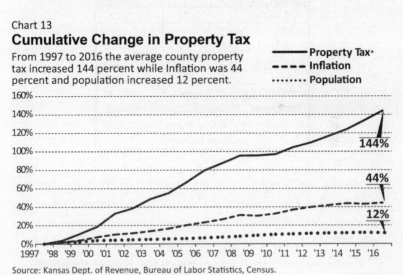

From 1997 to 2016 the average county property tax increased 144 percent while Inflation was 44 percent and population increased 12 percent.

— Property Tax*
- - - Inflation
······· Population

Source: Kansas Dept. of Revenue, Bureau of Labor Statistics, Census.
* County tax only, excludes all other jurisdictions

State budget pro forma reports of revenues and expenditures (called "profiles" in Kansas) are required to assume that anything in statute will occur, so deficits will continue to be inflated (or surpluses understated) until legislators remove dormant transfers from statute. And if you're wondering why this silly practice has continued for more than a decade, it's to avoid having to deal with criticism from local government officials and their lobbyists. LAVTR was intended to provide local property tax relief, but the compound annual growth rate for county property tax between 1998 and 2003 was a whopping 7.52 percent. Local government officials didn't provide any relief . . . they just spent more. Now, local government likes to partly blame property tax hikes on the legislature for not funding LAVTR and CCRS, and they most assuredly would criticize legislators for eliminating the statutory references to state tax dollars to which they still feel entitled.

Table 19: Phony Deficit Causes		
Transfer	FY 2021	FY 2022
LAVTR	$ -	$ 103.8
CCRS	$ 79.2	$ 80.7
Bioscience	$ 100.0	$ 100.0
Total	$ 179.2	$ 284.5

Source: KS Dept. of Revenue, KS Division of the Budget. Assumes a 2 percent annual increase in Sales & Use Tax on the FY 2019 Revenue Estimate.

By the way, legislators didn't remove those transfers from statute when they passed the FY 2018–2019 budget. Perhaps to avoid faux political high dudgeon from cities and counties ("How dare they strip from statute money we haven't received for more than ten years!"), the legislature merely deferred transfers for a short time. An analysis by the Kansas Division of the Budget says LAVTR was suspended until FY

2021, when $54 million would be transferred and the FY 2022 transfer would be 3.63 percent of retail sales and compensating use tax. City County Revenue Sharing begins again in FY 2021 at 2.823 percent of retail sales and compensating use tax, as does an estimated $100 million for the Bioscience transfer.[184] Left unchanged, these transfers could collectively prompt phony budget deficits of $179.2 million in FY 2021 and $284.5 million in FY 2022.

Citizens Opposed Most Tax Increases

It was clear from opening day that most lawmakers had a hunger for tax increases and no appetite for budget cuts, despite evidence that voters preferred the latter to the former. Three separate polls revealed a plurality of voters preferred using spending cuts to balance the state budget, rather than relying on tax increases. In the biannual Fort Hays State University Docking Institute survey, only a quarter of respondents wanted lawmakers to use tax increases to balance the budget.[185] An overwhelming majority wanted spending cuts or a combination of spending cuts and tax increases to fill any budget gaps.

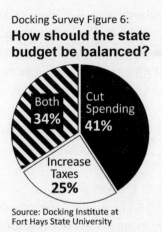

Docking Survey Figure 6:
How should the state budget be balanced?

Source: Docking Institute at
Fort Hays State University

A poll conducted by the Kansas Chamber of Commerce found 57 percent of Kansans said the budget should be balanced with spending cuts.[186] The Kansas Policy Institute poll gave participants options beyond cutting costs or raising taxes but still, their #1 preference for balancing the budget—38 percent—was to reduce the cost of government.[187]

"It's the will of the people" was one of the often-cited justifications for imposing the largest tax increase in Kansas history, but in reality, it was just the will of certain legislators, media, and special interests that profit from more government spending. The non-sequitur train-of-thought went something like this: "Many conservative legislators were voted out of office in 2016 . . . I was voted in and I want to raise taxes . . . therefore the people want me to raise taxes."

Teenager logic aside, those same three scientific market surveys determined that "the people" did NOT want their taxes increased. The Docking Institute survey showed that only 8 percent of Kansans supported a tax increase on the middle class and only 26 percent supported a tax increase on small business. Nearly half (46 percent) of Kansans believed taxes on small business and the middle class should have been decreased. The Kansas Chamber survey also showed strong opposition to a middle-class tax increase, with 77 percent opposed and only 17 percent in favor; that survey also showed only 24 percent favored raising taxes on small business. Just 4 percent of participants in the Kansas Policy Institute survey preferred a personal income tax as the primary method of balancing the budget and only 17 percent supported doing so by increasing the income tax on business.

A Tax Increase Wasn't Necessary

The facts overwhelmingly showed voters wanted spending reductions to be the primary means of balancing the budget and opposed personal income tax hikes, but most legislators weren't about to let voter sentiment get in the way of what they wanted to do.

Ronald Reagan could have been speaking of the 2017 Kansas legislative session when he said, "Government is like a baby. An alimentary canal with a big appetite at one end and no sense of responsibility at the other."

There were multiple options remaining near the end of the session to balance the budget, when house Appropriations had narrowed the two-year budget shortfall to $396 million. Securitizing (selling) future tobacco settlement revenues would generate at least $265 million each year. Collecting a royalty from the Kansas Turnpike Authority (a separate unit of state government) of 15 percent of toll revenue would increase revenue by $33 million over two years, and KTA could easily afford it; KTA's 2016 audited financial report shows they had a $37 million "profit" and finished the year with $120 million in cash and receivables.

There were also two other big options to reduce costs. Local school districts began the year with a record-setting $911 million in unencumbered cash reserves, much of which represented aid collected in prior years but not spent. The Alvarez & Marsal efficiency report recommended school cash reserves be limited to a maximum of 15 percent of current operating costs, with any excess being deducted from the following year's state funding. Based on 2016 spending, doing so would have produced a one-time savings of $196.5 million in FY 2018.

Table 20: Options to Balance the Budget without Tax Increases		
Description	FY 2018	FY 2019
Tobacco Securitization	$ 265.0	$ 265.0
Turnpike Royalty	$ 16.0	$ 17.0
K-12 Cash Reserves	$ 196.5	$ -
Spending reductions by Governor	$ 100.0	$ 100.0
Total	$ 577.5	$ 382.0

At the close of the 2016 session, the legislature required the governor to make spending reductions at the beginning of the next fiscal year, and the same could be done again. Reducing baseline costs by $100 million (about 3 percent of General Fund spending other than K–12) would produce $200 million in savings over two years. Some legislators believe costs could be reduced but say the budget system within the legislative cycle doesn't allow adequate time to get at the information they need, so giving the governor authority to cut costs outside of that cycle addresses that concern. Others, of course, believe spending couldn't possibly be cut even though Kansas spent 27 percent more per-resident than the states without an income tax in 2015, and coincidentally, had 27 percent more state employees than the national average.[188]

The combination of these revenue enhancements and spending reductions provided a $960 million menu of options to close a $396 million shortfall. The budget would have had healthy ending balances and a little left over to resolve the school funding issue even if only some of the options were implemented. Some of those options may not be ideal policy, but each would have been much better than foisting a large, unnecessary tax increase on citizens.

Brownback's 2017 Budget Proposal

Governor Brownback's 2017 budget proposal increased a number of taxes and fees to generate about $377 million in additional revenue. His budget was designed to add revenue by:

- Adding $1-per-pack tax hike on cigarettes
- Doubling the sales tax on tobacco from 10 percent to 20 percent
- Increasing the state liquor enforcement tax from 8 percent to 16 percent

- Imposing a tax on passive income silent partners receive in rents and royalties
- Increasing the for-profit business filing fee from $40 to $200.

Before adding new taxes and fees, Brownback asked lawmakers to look at increasing government efficiencies before asking individual Kansans to pay more. In his 2017 State of the State Address,[189] he suggested several opportunities to streamline government, including:

- Merging barbering and cosmetology licensing agencies
- Merging departments that regulate state insurance and securities markets.

"We owe it to Kansas taxpayers to find those efficiencies again, before asking for more revenue," Brownback told the Kansas legislature during the address on January 10, 2017. His budget proposal also suggested taking money from the Kansas Highway Fund and securitizing a long-term tobacco-settlement fund known as the Children's Initiative Fund, and temporarily transferring money from an unclaimed property fund.

Brownback said his budget used "modest, targeted revenue measures to fund essential state services."

The proposal was dead on arrival.

Within hours of Kansas Budget Director Shawn Sullivan presenting a detailed outline of the plan to house and senate panels, Republican leadership in the senate released a joint statement excoriating the proposal. The statement by Senate President Susan Wagle, Senate Vice President Jeff Longbine, Majority Leader Jim Denning, and Ways and Means Committee Chair Carolyn McGinn accused Brownback of kicking the can down the road.

"The governor continues to use one-time money, adds new taxes on the middle class, and neglects to fix the LLC loophole," the statement read. "The math simply doesn't add up. The solution will require a combination of cuts and changes to tax policy. Many members of the senate would rather see a long-term fix, and we expect to debate alternative proposals. We look forward to working with the house and the governor to reach a sustainable solution for all Kansans."

Despite the senate leadership suggestion that the alternative solutions would include budget cuts, no meaningful spending cuts made it into the final budget. Within a month, lawmakers in the house would pass a tax policy retroactively increasing income taxes by $2.4 billion over five years. The senate would follow suit. And despite their preaching on the evils of using one-time money, both chambers would eventually approve a budget heavily dependent upon one-time money to pay for huge spending increases.

Retroactive Tax Increase: Part 1
The senate Committee on Assessment and Taxation killed Brownback's budget proposal on Valentine's Day. Members refused to forward the bill out of committee for consideration by the full senate. The same day, committee members forwarded a Democratic plan to the senate that would add a new, third income tax bracket for 6.45 percent for single filers earning more than $35,000 and eliminate the LLC tax exemption.

That plan, SB 188,[190] garnered ten votes out of the forty-member senate, but senators would have another chance to vote on a tax plan within a few days.

As the senate shot down the Democratic tax plan, a large majority of the house, 76–48, passed HB 2178,[191] a retroactive income tax increase. HB 2178 eliminated the LLC-tax exemption. It included:

- A third tax rate of 5.45 percent up from 4.6 percent, affecting married people filing jointly who earn more than $100,000.
- A higher middle tax rate of 5.25 percent up from 4.6 percent, affecting married people filing jointly who earn between $30,000 and $100,000.
- A flat bottom tax rate of 2.7 percent for those who earn less than $30,000.

If adopted, the new rates and repeal of the pass-through exemption would be retroactive to January 1, 2017.

It was a rapid turn of events that put HB 2178 on the house floor, and no one rose to debate its merits prior to the vote. As Republican Rep. Erin Davis told the *Kansas City Star*,[192] "It was really interesting that we just passed a billion dollar tax increase in what, I don't know, 30 seconds or something like that?"

Senate leadership opted to skip over traditional means of advancing the legislation. Typically, the senate vets bills that pass through the house at such an early point in the legislative session. Senate President Susan Wagle opted instead to forgo committee hearings, a debate, and a vote in committee. Two days after the house passed HB 2178, the full senate voted 22–18 to accept the house bill without amendment. There was bipartisan support and opposition to the legislation. Even senate leadership was divided on the proposal.

Republican Sen. Jeff Longbine, the senate vice president, voted in favor of the retroactive tax increase, telling the *Star*[193] he didn't see a path for different legislation that would raise more revenue. Wagle said she voted against the bill because it didn't include spending cuts. However, she later tweeted that the governor should sign the legislation.

Five days later, Brownback wielded his veto pen. In a message[194] he submitted to legislators, Brownback said his veto was "based on the belief that, as the elected public servants of Kansas, we must not choose to resolve budget challenges on the backs of middle income Kansans with retroactive personal income tax increases . . . applying a retroactive tax increase on our citizens is irresponsible and will ultimately harm families and individuals who are working to make ends meet. Were this bill to become law, the majority of Kansans would see a significant reduction in their paycheck immediately. This is unfair. I also reject the idea that we must choose to either make large cuts to public education or burden every hard working Kansan with a higher tax rate. This dichotomy is false."

Within the hour, the house took up a vote to override Brownback's veto. Eighty-three house members voted to forward the bill to final action with eighty-four votes needed to override a veto. Going into the vote, it appeared the house needed only one person to flip in order to keep the legislation alive and override the veto. They got two. Rep. Clay Aurand, a Belleville Republican, walked to the well and said he saw no other alternatives.

"I see no other possibility, unfortunately. I'd like to change my vote and vote 'yes,'" he said as the floor erupted with cheers. Rep. Blaine Finch, an Ottawa Republican, also changed his vote saying he wanted to "send a strong message." With a final count of 85–40, the house overrode Brownback's veto with jubilee.[195] The celebration was short-lived.

The senate needed to find five votes to override but only secured two. Republican Sen. Elaine Bowers voted against the legislation initially, but voted to override the governor's veto. Democratic Sen. Tom Holland did the same. Senate leadership was divided on the best path forward. Vice President Longbine voted to override the veto. Senate President Susan Wagle said Brownback had put Republicans in a bad position, but she voted to sustain the veto. Senate Majority Leader Jim Denning said he couldn't vote for the override, because the bill was retroactive. However, Denning called the governor's budget plan "insulting," as he cast his vote to allow the veto to stand.

An Early Train

"This isn't the last train out of the station," Denning assured the senate before voting against the veto override. It was an early train, but the tax bills that immediately followed HB 2178 didn't see many passengers.

Proposals to increase the cigarette tax withered in committees. Brownback said he would be willing to sign legislation to flatten income tax rates. He issued a statement signaling his support for SB 214, a bill that would set a flat 4.6 percent income tax rate.

"My goal has always been to make Kansas the best state in America to raise a family and grow a business. A flat tax accomplishes this goal by making taxes fair for everyone and encouraging economic growth. The senate's flat tax legislation creates a single low tax rate for Kansans, solving today's budget challenges without unnecessarily harming economic growth in Kansas. If the legislature sends a bill to my desk similar in nature to SB 214, I will sign it."[196]

Even before the vote, it looked like tickets for the SB 214 train would be a hard sell in the senate.

"Could I laugh any harder?" Republican Sen. Barbara Bollier told the *Wichita Eagle*,[197] signaling moderates were unlikely to support the bill.

Conservatives, who in seasons past championed the idea of a flatter tax code, also balked at the suggestion, and Democrats were never willing to board the flat tax train. House Minority Leader Jim Ward called it a "fundamentally terrible idea."[198]

When the proposal reached the senate floor, few wanted on that train. It was derailed with a decisive 3–37 vote. In the house, a proposal for a flat, 5 percent income tax rate[199] coupled with eliminating sales tax on food, and scrapping the LLC-tax exemption, earned enough votes in the house Taxation Committee to be forwarded to the full house for consideration, but the house never debated the bill.

Speaker of the House Ron Ryckman in a 2017 interview said until the senate torpedoed its flat tax bill, the house bill looked like something that could pass. Ryckman actively whipped votes on the house measure. With the governor on board, Ryckman needed only sixty-three votes. Though competing factions in the house—the Democrats, self-described moderate Republicans, and conservatives—weren't excited about the legislation, Ryckman thought he could cobble together the votes until the senate bill imploded.

"Three votes [in the senate]. That's impossible to overcome," Ryckman said. There was no point in chasing votes for a bill that couldn't get senate support.

The house moved on to behind-the-scenes discussions for a two-tier tax plan that would have increased rates from 2.7 to 3 percent on the bottom and from 4.6 percent to 5 percent on the top. Meanwhile, a loose coalition of about forty conservatives, the Truth Caucus, floated a proposal to craft a budget that didn't require tax increases. They called their plan the Republican Balanced Budget Solution.[200] The proposal would partially securitize the Children's Initiative Fund, and eliminate all proposed new spending in 2018 and 2019. Republicans Sen. Ty Masterson and Rep. Chuck Webber announced the plan in a press conference flanked by about a dozen lawmakers.

"As we approach Memorial Day, those controlling this legislature are no closer to a solution than they were in January," Masterson said. "As they work behind the scenes to reach the magic number of votes necessary to ram through a plan that includes new and unnecessary spending and pays for that new spending with higher taxes on the middle class, we have a simple, straightforward plan that balances our budget without increasing the burden on hard-working Kansans."

Like the proposals before it, the Republican Balanced Budget Solution train never left the station. Other tax proposals—one to eliminate sales tax on groceries and one to revoke sales tax exemptions on some services—faltered in the house. Meanwhile, legislative committees failed to forward to the chambers any proposals that created efficiencies and reduced spending.

Sacred Cow Drives the Train

If the Kansas budget is a train, the conductor is K–12 education. As Kansas Budget Director Shawn Sullivan said, school funding is the "sacred cow." Funding for Kansas schools comprises about 50 percent of the state General Fund budget and additional funding is provided through other state budgets. US Census data shows Kansas provided the sixth highest share of total school funding provided through the state budget for 2015.[201] Kansas schools receive 66 percent of funding from state government and 26 percent from local sources (mostly property taxes), whereas the national average is almost an equal split—47 percent from state funding and 45 percent from local sources. Federal funding comprises 8 percent of total funding in Kansas and also for the national average.

Table 21: 2015 School Funding Split		
State	**Kansas**	**National Avg.**
State share	66%	47%
Local share	26%	45%
Federal share	8%	8%
total	100%	100%
Source: U.S. Census		

State funding increased every year under Governor Brownback except for a small decline in 2016 when some pension funding was partially deferred, but that also commensurately reduced school costs so there was no net effect on schools.[202] Pension funding was the source of considerable controversy, with education lobbyists and other special interests claiming that funding only increased because of higher pension costs, but that was another myth. Spending per-pupil with pension funding excluded set an all-time record in 2017 at $12,687 based on data provided by the Kansas Department of Education and published by Kansas Policy Institute.[203]

School Year	State	Federal	Local	Total
2010	$ 6,326	$ 1,603	$ 4,406	$ 12,330
2011	$ 6,511	$ 1,465	$ 4,306	$ 12,283
2012	$ 6,983	$ 981	$ 4,692	$ 12,656
2013	$ 6,984	$ 1,005	$ 4,792	$ 12,781
2014	$ 7,088	$ 1,053	$ 4,819	$ 12,960
2015	$ 8,567	$ 1,101	$ 3,469	$ 13,124
2016	$ 8,540	$ 1,049	$ 3,444	$ 13,033
2017	$ 8,714	$ 1,082	$ 3,442	$ 13,237
2018 est.	$ 9,113	$ 1,054	$ 3,479	$ 13,647

Table 22: Per-Pupil Aid by Revenue Source

Source: Kansas Department of Education, based on full time equivalent enrollment. Beginning in 2015, aid erroneously recorded as Local in prior years is reflected as State aid, accounting for roughly $1,250 per-pupil.

Even though funding continued to increase, a lawsuit claiming funding was constitutionally inadequate filed by Kansas school districts on the day Governor Brownback was elected in 2010 ran through district court and the State Supreme Court even beyond the 2017 legislative session. The many absurdities of court rulings, false and misleading claims by education lobbyists, and the state's weak messaging on the realities of school funding, created continued pressure to ignore many school efficiency opportunities and increase funding. Brandon Smith, Brownback's policy director from 2015 forward, said he worried about the threat from the Kansas Supreme Court when discussing K–12 with the governor.

"Any big change to K–12 or reduction or forced efficiencies, in my mind, would necessarily ask for retaliation from the court," Smith said. "And that was always kind of a fear that if we got too aggressive with forcing efficiencies to K–12, or doing something that would be construed as cutting K–12, the courts would backlash immediately with a larger demand for an increased, specified dollar amount—which ironically, they may do anyways here in a couple of months." (A Kansas Supreme Court ruling on adequacy was pending at the time of Smith's interview in the summer of 2017.)

Governor Brownback did propose two pieces of legislation to create efficiencies in school spending. One bill, HB 2142,[204] would have created a school employee health benefit plan. Based on a recommendation from the Alvarez & Marsal efficiency study commissioned by the Kansas legislature in 2015, a statewide health plan would save the state $40 million in 2018 and another $80 million in 2019.

The bill met immediate resistance from the Kansas National Educators Association and other powerful lobbies.

Mark Desetti, KNEA lobbyist, wrote that the bill requires a high deductible insurance plan, guaranteeing that savings "will come out of employee's pockets. Employees then are left with fewer health benefits and no opportunity to offset the loss of benefits with an increase in salary. This plan truly represents a $25 million reduction in compensation for school employees across the state."[205]

The legislation bounced from house committee to house committee. The K–12 Education Budget Committee scheduled and then cancelled a hearing on the bill before referring it to the Appropriations Committee. Appropriations sent the bill back to the K–12 Education Budget Committee where it languishes at this writing. Lawmakers could take it up in 2018, but that seems unlikely.

The Alvarez & Marsal efficiency study also proposed saving money through group purchasing. HB 2143[206] would require Kansas's 280-plus school districts to procure IT equipment, food, and fuel as group purchases through the Department of Administration. Over two years, the bill would save $16 million, according to estimates. The K–12 Education Budget Committee hosted a hearing. Opposition was fierce. The Kansas Association of School Boards lobbyist told the committee the estimated savings could not be confirmed, some school districts already used joint purchasing, and that the policy would revoke local control, damaging local economies in the process.[207] The Beloit School District superintendent,[208] an Olathe Public Schools official,[209] and lobbyists for Wichita Public Schools[210] echoed those concerns with testimony.

Of seventeen submitted testimonies, only three offered support for the legislation, and a handful offered neutral testimony. It wasn't only school districts and school lobbies that voiced their opposition; much of the farm lobby did as well. The Kansas Cooperative Council and Agribusiness Retailers Association said the bill runs "counter to the intent of economic initiatives advanced in recent years by the legislature and the administration to encourage business growth in smaller communities."[211] A representative from the Harvey County Food and Farm Council worried the legislation would prevent local school districts from purchasing fresh tomatoes or asparagus from area farmers markets.[212] A board member with the High Plains Food Cooperative expressed concerns that the law would hurt family farms that now supply food to school districts to make up for declines in commodity prices.[213]

Farm and education lobbies actively opposed efficiencies in school district procurement policy even though the savings would mean more money available for instruction, so what little political will existed to save money through that efficiency evaporated. After the hearing, the committee referred the proposal to Appropriations. That committee later referred it back to the K–12 Education Budget Committee, where it languishes at this writing, pending possible recommendations from a working group of officials from school districts and the Department of Administration. Regardless of the rationale, objections to getting the same quality products and services at better prices are conscious decisions to place a higher priority on something other than educating students.

Retroactive Tax Increase: The Sequel
With the biggest potential money-saving proposals off the legislative table, a lot of empty tax and budget trains passing through the station with too few riders, and the legislative clock winding down, lawmakers appeared at an impasse. Republican house and senate leadership negotiated with Governor Brownback seeking a resolution. They needed a simple majority in both chambers and the governor or a two-thirds majority without the governor.

Lawmakers in both chambers settled on a proposal for a retroactive tax increase that raised $1.2 billion in new revenue in two years. Using the shell of a bill stuck in conference committee, lawmakers proposed legislation that eliminated the pass-through exemption and added a third-tier income tax rate for top earners. The policy increased the bottom rate from 2.7 percent to 2.9 percent in year one, and then to 3.1 percent the following year. The middle rate increased from 4.6 percent to 4.9 percent in year one to 5.25 percent in year two. The newly created top rate is 5.25 percent in year one and 5.7 percent thereafter. Taxpayers at all income levels were hit with double-digit rate hikes over two years, although the rate increases for those who itemize will be partially offset by the phase-in of deductions for mortgage interest and medical expenses (50 percent in 2017 and 2018, 75 percent in 2019, and 100 percent in 2020). Legislators also modified a provision that exempted tens of thousands of citizens from having to pay income tax; previous law exempted the first $5,000 of taxable income for single filers and the first $12,500 for married filers; those exemptions were reduced to $2,500 and $5,000 respectively.

Table 23: New Marginal Tax Rates					
Married Filing Jointly					
Taxable Income	**2017 Original Rate**	**2017 New Rate**	**2018 New Rate**	**2017 Retroactive Increase**	**2018 Increase Over 2016**
$0-$30,000	2.70%	2.90%	3.10%	7%	15%
$30,001- $60,000	4.60%	4.90%	5.25%	7%	14%
Over $60,000	4.60%	5.20%	5.70%	13%	24%
Single					
Taxable Income	**2017 Original Rate**	**2017 New Rate**	**2018 New Rate**	**2017 Retroactive Increase**	**2018 Increase Over 2016**
$0-$15,000	2.70%	2.90%	3.10%	7%	15%
$15,001- $30,000	4.60%	4.90%	5.25%	7%	14%
Over $30,000	4.60%	5.20%	5.70%	13%	24%
Source: Kansas Legislative Research					

Don't be fooled by claims that taxes are still lower than in 2012. The marginal rates may be lower but the sales tax and cigarette tax increases instituted since then remain in place. An analysis conducted by the Kansas Department of Revenue put the net effect of all tax changes between 2012 and 2016 resulted in only a $393 million tax reduction for Fiscal Year 2018; the $591 million Kansas income-tax hike imposed for Fiscal Year 2018 means citizens will be $198 million worse off on net than in 2012.[214]

For years, moderate Republicans and Democrats angrily accused conservatives of balancing the budget on the backs of the poor and middle-income families but once they regained power, they had no problem doing exactly that.

The tax increase marked the single, largest tax increase in Kansas history. The senate adopted the conference committee report for the bill with twenty-six votes, shy one vote of those necessary to override a veto. It was a tougher sell in the house. Only sixty-nine house members approved the committee report—nineteen votes shy of a veto-proof majority. The legislation was presented to the governor on June 6 and vetoed the same day.

Brownback met with a small group of legislators before lawmakers voted to override his veto. What happened in that meeting may have been the tipping point for some lawmakers who had been hesitant to vote in favor of the tax increase.

Republican Rep. Dan Hawkins told the *Kansas City Star* he called the meeting hoping to find a tax plan all Republicans could support.[215] According to the *Star*, Brownback was asked if he was ready for the train that was about to roll over him if he refused to sign the tax bill, and Brownback told lawmakers it might be better politically to be hit by that train than sign a tax increase.

Brownback tells a slightly different story. According to the governor, Speaker Ryckman said he could cobble together enough conservatives to limit the top income tax rate to 5.3 percent, if the governor would agree to sign it. Otherwise, the top rate would be 5.7 with enough votes to override Brownback's veto.

"I don't believe in increasing income taxes," Brownback said.

He said he told house leadership he wasn't willing to sign a 5.3 percent tax increase, though he was willing to sign some increases to consumption taxes or other fees and put a cap on the LLC-exemption.

"So in that sense, [Ryckman] is accurate, where he said I'm not willing to do that," Brownback said. "And it would just be override my veto then."

Republican Sen. Richard Wilborn switched his vote in the senate to override the governor's veto. It was a taller hill to climb in the house, but several Representatives who met with the governor earlier in the day switched their votes, including Ryckman and Reps. Hawkins and Davis. Reps. Kristey Williams and Brenda Landwehr, who also attended the meeting, voted against overriding Brownback's veto. It wasn't enough. At final tally, eighty-eight house members, Republicans and Democrats, voted to end the LLC-exemption and increase income taxes on all Kansans.

As many news organizations would go on to report, it marked the end of the Brownback tax experiment. However, Brownback doesn't view it as a total loss. For five years, he noted, Kansas policy was the top tax story in America. The conversation is ongoing, and now, Brownback thinks other states and specifically the federal government will have data to support their efforts to lower taxes.

Brownback sees Kansas as the pioneer. "This is the piece I feel great about for us," the governor said. "I feel like the old saying has come true that the pioneers get the arrows and the settlers the land."

Kansas did pioneer the emphasis on pass-through employers; the importance of their contribution to the national jobs picture and the nation's dependence upon jobs created by new establishments helped inform proposals to significantly reduce the federal income tax on pass-through companies instead of just C-corporations.

Other states (e.g., North Carolina, Indiana, Tennessee, Wisconsin), however, successfully reduced marginal tax rates. Kansas has been made the poster child for not cutting taxes, yet tax reform didn't fail because taxes cannot be reduced, but because of a long list of mostly self-inflicted issues.

7

Lessons Learned

"The worst thing that can happen to a good cause is, not to be skillfully attacked, but to be poorly defended."
—Frederic Bastiat

One of the most common questions asked about the Kansas tax-relief effort goes like this: "A lot of people are saying the Kansas experience is a warning to other states about the perils of cutting taxes. What do you say to that?" And the answer is, "Of course, no state should be like Kansas; who in their right mind would cut taxes *and* increase spending?"

That's one of the greater mistakes made in Kansas, but there are many other important lessons to be learned in three major areas: planning, communication, and procedural/operational. Developing and implementing tax relief is the focus of the following lessons learned, but they also apply to a wide range of policy and operational matters.

Lesson #1—Know Where You're Going and Get Everyone On Board

The tax reformers had the best of intentions, but they didn't have a comprehensive long-term plan to bring spending in line with adjusted revenue, and the rationale for tax reduction was not clear to citizens. In *It's Not What You Say . . . It's What You Do*, author Laurence Haughton writes, "Good managers at every level recognize the importance of strategic planning and setting concrete goals for their employees. But even the best among them often fail to implement and support the crucial processes that turn well-laid plans into visible successes. Studies show that over the last fifty years, a whopping 83 percent of corporate slowdowns were attributable not to outside economic forces but to the lack of vigilant follow-through within the company itself."[216]

The subtitle of the book is "How Following Through at Every Level Can Make or Break Your Company," but his points also apply to government. Haughton recommends these four critical Building Blocks:

1. Clear Direction
2. The Right People
3. Buy-In
4. Individual Initiative

There was very little that was clear about the tax-relief plan, including how the changes would impact individual taxpayers. In addition to reducing marginal tax rates, the 2012 plan and the 2013 plan changes also adjusted the standard deduction allowance, deductions for those who itemize, and some tax credits. Clarity was also absent on the rationale for reducing taxes and for the short-term and longer-term economic expectations. It's not enough to say, for example, that more jobs will be created with lower taxes; voters and legislators must be uncomfortably aware of the unseen consequences of *not* taking action.

Lack of clarity on the need for change plays into one of the key Buy-In elements, which Haughton calls outmaneuvering the CAVE people (Citizens Against Virtually Everything).[217] He writes, "Just as our bodies have an immune system that assaults everything new and unfamiliar, organizations have their own auto-immune response that instinctively and impulsively attacks every new idea, novel solution and call for change. Overtly and covertly, these antibodies in human form (aka the CAVE people) chip away at your team's willingness to trust and try new things, poisoning the environment in order to keep necessary changes from taking hold."

Public policy changes are not just subject to attack from the internal "team" of agency managers, employees, and legislators. The CAVE people also include media and every special interest group fearing, in this case, that its funding might be constrained.

Some CAVE people are easily identifiable, but not all, and it's important to know where everyone stands. At the beginning of the 2017 legislative session, Kansas Policy Institute asked all 165 Kansas legislators to declare their principles on key budget and education issues in a voluntary online survey. One question asked whether their primary focus of balancing the budget would be (a) reduce spending through efficiency, (b) raise income taxes on citizens, (c) raise income taxes on business, or (d) some other tax or fee. Only thirty-four legislators responded to the survey; twenty-eight said they would reduce spending through efficiency, five said they would increase taxes, and one did not answer this question. The majority of legislators might say they believe in making good use of taxpayer money, but when they won't declare it as a guiding principle, your economic freedom is likely subordinate to special interest demands for higher taxes.

Tips and Tactics

- Develop a guiding set of principles for tax and budget policy; share those principles with the public and reference them frequently (especially when responding to questions and criticism). The American Legislative Exchange Council's Principles of Taxation is a great reference point.[218]
- Identify the guiding principles of key players.
- Identify and quantify the problem to be resolved, as well as potential consequences of *not* resolving the problem.

- Build consensus with citizens and legislators on the nature and severity of the problem long before introducing the solution. People are much more likely to buy your product if they believe they need it. And learn from the objections and questions raised; it's always best to know the objections ahead of time so you can constructively address them and play offense rather than defense.

- Settle on clearly defined desired outcomes before building the plan (or as Yogi might say, decide where you're going before thinking about how you'll get there).

- Avoid the political temptation to promise that improvement will come quickly. Change takes time, and often much more time than one might anticipate. Change also doesn't happen in a vacuum; while Kansas was cutting taxes, Obamacare taxes and mandates kicked in and then oil and agriculture prices tanked.

- Give at least one team member absolute permission and the responsibility to challenge any element of the plan, especially anything that goes against principles or is likely to be misunderstood.

Lesson #2—Win the Battle for Citizens' Minds

In 1981, Al Ries and Jack Trout wrote what some people believe is the most influential advertising book ever written: *Positioning: The Battle for Your Mind.* In the twentieth-anniversary edition, Ries and Trout share one of the most critical insights on success in advertising, and it's just as important in the policy and legislative arena. They say, "Truth is irrelevant. What matters are the perceptions that exist in the mind. The essence of positioning thinking is to accept the perceptions as reality and then restructure those perceptions to create the position you desire."[219]

Much of what has been written about the Kansas tax-relief effort has been inaccurate, incomplete, or misrepresented—and in some cases, deliberately so. Ries and Trout teach us that simply declaring, "That's wrong!" will have no positive effect on minds that already believe otherwise, yet that was often the go-to reaction from many tax-relief proponents. Even worse, it was not unusual for false or misleading claims to go unchallenged; the thinking was: "What's the use? The media will just say whatever they want."

But even if that's the case, letting false and misleading statements go unchallenged only accomplishes two things: false perceptions are reinforced and bad behavior is emboldened. Preparation is essential when trying to restructure perceptions, and having a well-constructed strategic messaging plan allows for rapid response.

The essence of an effective strategic messaging plan lies in that old advertising adage—facts tell but stories sell. Facts that are relevant and relatable to the typical audience member are absolutely needed, but they need to be presented as reinforcement to a compelling story or to restructure perceptions. For example, it's a fact that nine states do not have a personal income tax, but "other states do it and we can, too" doesn't change minds. The CAVE people easily pushed back on that fact with a compelling, but utterly false, response. "Yes, some states don't have an income tax, but they have advantages that don't exist in Kansas, and that's why they can get by without an income tax. Texas has oil, Florida has tourism, and Nevada has gambling, for example. Kansas doesn't have those attributes so we can't eliminate our income tax." Minds disinclined to change can easily latch onto that explanation as justification for maintaining the status quo.

Relatable facts sprinkled into a persuasive story can allow the audience to walk away from a previously held belief, without being told they are wrong. "You know, I've heard that, too. But I also read something that looked into that theory. Every state provides the same basic services, right? Education, social services, highways, etc. But the states that tax income spend 42 percent more per capita than the states without an income tax . . . providing those same basic services. Texas could have all the oil in nation and still have a high tax burden if they spent a lot more. But they and the other states provide those services at a lower cost, and that's what allows them to have lower taxes. They spend less, so they can tax less."

Kevan Kjar and Kelly Shaw literally wrote the book on storytelling. *The ArrowHead: Winning the Story War* actually teaches how to create messages with purpose, passion, and power by telling a book-length story that enlightens and inspires.[220]

Kjar said, "The ArrowHead, simply put, is a perfect metaphor for the moral of your product's best story with a hero, and enough backstory to make it compelling and convincing in fifteen seconds. An arrow, like a great message, flies straight and penetrates; it requires a sharp point to penetrate the heart, and is supported by a shaft of compelling data to give it weight and credibility. An ArrowHead is your unique selling proposition, where you have an unfair competitive advantage over your nearest competitor.

"The ArrowHead is not just knowing what your best message and story IS, more importantly it is knowing what your best message and story IS NOT. Created by a cross-functional team of your experts, the ArrowHead comes from a cauldron of analysis, discussion, debate, brainstorming, testing, fine-tuning and consensus. The rigorous nature of the ArrowHead creation process develops a passionate and united coalition because your team knows what it took to get there."

Commenting on the book, Dirk Bak, CEO and president of Corporate Facilities Management, Inc. said, "The ArrowHead is a modern day masterpiece for all executives who have ever lost a deal and witnessed an opportunity slip away."[221] That perfectly describes the Kansas tax-relief effort—an opportunity that slipped away, largely because the messaging was ceded to tax-relief opponents.

The key players in the Brownback administration and the legislature were aware that Kansas had been suffering long-term out-migration; they knew that job growth was far below the national average, the productivity gap was getting worse, and that those ongoing factors would exacerbate an already bleak state budget picture due to burgeoning costs for pensions and Medicaid. Most Kansans and legislators, however, had no idea what was on the horizon because the cold hard facts hadn't been laid out. Maybe it was assumed there was already sufficient awareness of those challenges, or maybe the tax reformers wanted to avoid talking about harsh realities and just focus on the upside. It's natural to resist change, however, and failure to create a strong sense of urgency on the need for change left voters and legislators vulnerable to false claims that change would cause service cuts.

How one goes about creating that sense of urgency is of utmost importance. It's far more effective to help your audience reach their own informed decisions rather than try to "sell" them on your belief, as described in this column published in *State Policy Network Magazine*.[222]

When Kansas Policy Institute launched its school choice initiative in early 2010, I was trying to convince people that school choice was a good way to address low achievement scores, focusing on the National Assessment of Education Progress data. I was appalled that only 35 percent of 4th grade students in Kansas were Proficient in Reading. We at Kansas Policy Institute knew school choice was a major part of Florida's success in raising NAEP scores, so off I went, determined to generate interest in school choice by helping Kansans understand the truth about student achievement.

Progress, at first, was almost non-existent. Then, I

remembered something from my days in advertising: Nobody likes salespeople, and nobody likes it when you try to sell them something that they don't believe they need. So I stopped trying to "sell" policy and became a policy counselor. That was an important point for me to remember.

We've all seen the studies showing that people like their schools. That fondness may be based on faulty information, but we won't have much success telling people they are wrong. Instead, we have to help them change their minds by giving them permission to abandon a previously held belief.

I shared this idea with my colleagues, that of being a counselor versus a salesman, and we began modifying our approach. Now, in the course of establishing some baseline facts about a local school district (we never go in with the stated purpose of talking about school choice), we show how the students in that district perform on the state assessment test. We're not talking about some abstract numbers for the entire state—we're talking about their kids.

For example, in the Wichita district, we'd show that 35 percent of 11th grade students "read grade-appropriate material with full comprehension" and then ask: "Is that acceptable?" It doesn't matter whether the number is 35, 50 or 65 percent, the audience always says the same thing: "Of course not." Before long, someone follows up with, "What can we do?"

"Selling" policy ideas comes off as trying to convince people that we're right and they might be wrong, and that's a tough proposition. But posing questions that ask people to make their own value judgments is a powerful way to advance good policy.

We take the position that there really is no "right" or "wrong" on policy (facts, yes, but not policy); saying that policy decisions are subjective choices allows people to engage in a discussion, not a sales pitch. We explain that our role is to give people facts so they can make their own informed decisions. It's much easier to connect emotionally when you give people permission to make their own decisions. Tell them that if they believe the status quo is acceptable, there's no need to change; but if not, here's a menu of possible changes to consider. Of course, everyone resists change but don't let them "off the couch." Ask for acknowledgment that they're accepting the status quo.

Allowing people to make their own decisions and telling them there is no right or wrong on policy matters also helps build credibility, especially when someone tries to shout you down claiming that there most definitely is a right position—and it's not yours. Your opponent just made you the adult in the room.

Part of giving the audience permission to abandon a previously held belief is avoiding the temptation to assess blame. Once someone asks, "What can we do?" keep going forward and focus on possible solutions. The answer to "Whose fault is this?" is "Even if we could agree on that, it wouldn't change anything. Let's just say it's no one's fault but everyone's responsibility."

Most often, disagreements over policy issues are based in emotion, not facts. We might argue about certain facts, but deep down, there's probably an emotional driver. Emotion-based arguments are never won by facts. Communicating as a counselor helps make the necessary emotional connections that are essential to advancing good policy. Once connected, it's much easier to have an adult conversation about the facts.

A campaign to win the battle for citizens' minds on the need for tax cuts might have started with several weeks of informational messages laying out the facts about systemic out-migration of population and Adjusted Gross Income, sub-standard job growth, and looming budgetary challenges. Personal appearances at town hall meetings and with editorial boards by key members of the administration and legislators could follow, explaining why the concept of cutting taxes seems to be a viable solution to multiple economic challenges; these are also opportunities to gather feedback on possible ways to construct a tax-relief plan.

The CAVE people will come out in force and those are opportunities that can be turned to your advantage. Don't play defense—make them play defense by asking questions.

"Aren't you troubled by sub-standard job growth and population loss?"

[Of course.]

"Well, if you don't like this solution, what's yours?"

[Typically, more "investment" in education, transportation, etc.]

"So let me get this straight . . . your solution to improving citizens' prosperity is to take more money from them so government can spend more?"

The CAVE people typically don't have solutions—just objections. With the proper preparation, you can help the audience see who is trying to solve their problems. And with the economic challenges established, you can persistently meet objections to change in a way that puts the onus on intransigents. "So you don't like this solution and if you don't have a viable option to propose, does that mean you're okay with sub-standard job growth and population loss?"

Knowing how to communicate your plan in ways that are meaningful to your audience is obviously critical, but one must also know how to effectively position the opposition. That's the key to winning the battle for citizens' minds.

Tips and Tactics

- Never promise or predict something that cannot be easily and undeniably proven to the typical citizen, such as a tax cut "will pay for itself."

- Be realistic about timelines. People and businesses will respond to tax cuts but it takes time. Political exuberance (e.g., Governor Brownback's predictions that the tax cut would be "a shot of adrenaline to the economy") quickly becomes a club with which opponents and media will mercilessly beat you.

- Anticipate the objections and criticisms and get there first. Don't wait to play defense.

- So much opposition is based on false understanding of the issues, so seek and embrace opportunities to address unfriendly audiences. It's important to hear objections that aren't filtered through media and special interests and at the very least, you'll gain grudging respect for having the courage and conviction for civilly engaging on the issues.

- Invite opposition leaders to join you in public discussions of the issues. If the Kansas experience is any guide, opponents will refuse to civilly discuss issues where they can be publicly held accountable. Refusal to engage is another opportunity to exploit; hold the event and leave an empty chair on stage for effect. And you still win if they agree to debate.

- Show humility. If a mistake is made or something doesn't turn out as planned, lean into it and own it. Citizens are far more forgiving of a politician who admits an error than one who tries to ignore it or explain it away.

- Firmly and professionally call out false or misleading statements. Many such instances were ignored in Kansas, thinking that the perpetrators' minds couldn't be changed or media was biased (which was most often true). But the perpetrators shouldn't be the only target of your response; these are opportunities to talk around them and speak directly to the public. Let those whose minds aren't quite made up see you as the adult in the room.

- Messaging must be consistent and relentless. When the team is weary of repeating why the plan is necessary, explaining the key elements and debunking the same false claim over and over again, your message is only beginning to sink in with the audience.

Lesson #3—Remove Organizational and Procedural Barriers

Failure to match spending with tax revenue was the ultimate undoing of the Kansas tax-relief effort, and while a good bit of that was political in nature, there were many organizational and procedural issues that complicated the budget process. Kansas has a part-time legislature that is scheduled for a single ninety-day session each year, but the actual time to analyze spending is less than that. Committees don't normally meet on "Pro Forma" days (often Fridays early in the session) or when legislators are engaged in day-long floor debate. Published committee calendars show the house Appropriations Committee met just thirty-five times during the 2017 legislative session and the senate Ways and Means only met thirty-one times, with most meetings lasting between one and two hours.[223] Committee members also participate on sub-committees that meet separately with agencies, but there is still not enough time available to conduct a thorough analysis of spending and performance metrics of programs and services.

Legislators need good data in addition to having adequate time for review, but that's often lacking. Insufficient data, little time to review and political hesitancy to cut is a potent recipe for a lot of unnecessary and inefficient spending. Representative Kasha Kelley noted the difference between building a budget and doling out money during a house Appropriations Committee hearing a few years ago, saying, "Sir, we do not have a budget process in Kansas; we have an appropriations process."

The *State Budget Reform Toolkit* published by the American Legislative Exchange Council (ALEC) advances a set of budget and procurement best practices to guide state policymakers.[224] Priority-based budgeting (also known as performance-based or results-based) is one of their key recommendations, which requires each agency and the legislature to prioritize every program or service from most to least effective. ALEC's Bob Williams, a former state legislator, former member of the General Accountability Office, and then president of State Budget Solutions, provided the following description of priority-based budgeting in a paper published by Kansas Policy Institute.[225]

> Budgets drive all policy, which is why debating, writing, and approving a state budget is the primary task legislators must accomplish. Many state legislators start the budget process by taking existing programs, adjusting costs for inflation, adding caseload increases, splicing in a few new initiatives, and—calling this their baseline budget. In this model cost, effectiveness and demand for existing programs is rarely considered.
>
> Legislators should junk the old conventional model and start designing budgets from the ground up based on priorities and performance.
>
> Priorities are determined by well-defined core functions: What is government responsible for achieving? Performance is the measure of how efficiently and effectively those priorities are delivered

Priority-based budgeting views all of state government—all of its agencies and functions—as a single enterprise. New proposals are evaluated in the context of all that state government is responsible for doing, and the strategies for achieving the best results are developed with an eye on all of the state's resources. Agencies and services are all under one tent where they can be constantly evaluated to ensure they are delivering the highest priorities as efficiently and effectively as possible.

Priority-based budgeting prompts governors and legislators to ask four key questions at the start of each legislative session:

- What must the state accomplish?
- How will the state measure its progress and success?
- How much money does the state have available to spend?
- What is the most efficient and effective way to deliver essential services within available funds?

Question #1: What must the state accomplish?

The first step in responsible budgeting is to determine the state's core functions: the essential services it must deliver to citizens, in priority order. We suggest developing a meaningful list of no more than ten core government functions.

Once the core functions are determined, they should serve as a litmus test for the hundreds of agencies, boards, commissions, programs and services currently being funded, as well as all future proposals. Agencies should be asked to submit their budgets based on delivering one or more of the state's identified core functions. If an agency or program is not advancing one of these functions, it should be abolished.

Question #2: How will states measure progress or success?

After identifying the state's core functions, legislatures must define specific and measurable results to be achieved, as well as benchmarks to measure progress toward those results.

Once the state and agencies have defined what it looks like to successfully achieve government's core functions, legislators must determine how to measure progress toward those outcomes. Performance indicators are a key tool to make accountability possible by allowing legislators and agencies to answer the question: "Are we making progress toward our goals?"

Question #3: How much money does the state have available to spend?

States should not spend or plan to spend more than the forecasted revenue for the next budget period. We recommend forming a non-partisan revenue forecast council to provide a bottom line before budget discussion begins.

Question #4: What is the most efficient and effective way to deliver essential services within available funds?

This question is about making sure essential services are delivered as efficiently and effectively as possible without compromising on cost and quality.

Once agencies have submitted a budget, legislative policy committees should carefully review all agency priorities and budget requests under their jurisdiction to determine whether or not they comply with core functions of government that have been adopted.

As lawmakers review agency goals and confirm they are core functions, they should consider whether government must actually deliver the services that accomplish those goals, or whether government's duty is simply to ensure the goals are accomplished. (See privatization section).

Essentially priorities-based budgeting changes the budget submission rules. Agency budgets become less about requesting funding, and more about offering to deliver specific results for a specific price.

Priorities-based budgeting serves citizens well by ensuring government delivers essential services as efficiently and effectively as possible. It maximizes the value of each hard-earned tax dollar, which is an important responsibility of legislators. It protects vulnerable programs from election-year rhetoric. It provides a logical place to begin meaningful debate and restructure spending.

The Kansas legislature finally approved a performance-based budgeting process in 2016, directing the legislative and executive branches "to cooperate in developing a revised budget process that will inventory all state programs and prioritize, identify the authority for, and develop a system of outcome-based performance measures for those programs on or before January 14, 2019."[226] One can only wonder how much better the tax-relief effort would have fared if a well-designed performance-based system had been in place a decade earlier.

Hiding money from the budget process is another way spending gets out of control in Kansas—and probably in most states. Kansas, for example, has statutory requirements to transfer 16.154 percent of retail sales tax receipts and compensating use tax receipts directly to the state highway fund.[227] Consequently, $514.5 million in 2017 sales and use tax revenue does not flow through the General Fund for appropriation to determine whether all or a portion of that money needs to be spent on highways. And money transferred in is routinely not scrutinized for necessity of spending, partly because the statutory specification is seen as "blessing" the spending—which is why legislators should eliminate all transfers and put every penny of spending through a rigorous priority-based budget review process. (FYI, Kansas has transferred large portions of the highway sales tax back to the General Fund for many years just to balance the budget and not because of any rigorous spending review.)

Finally, it's important that legislators and citizens alike have a firm understanding of key economic trends.

Tips and Tactics

- Implement a rigorous priority-based budget process.
- Eliminate transfers and statutory spending; put every penny through the priority-based review.
- Ensure adequate time to review data from the priority-based system by having budget committees meet year-round.
- Examine the revenue estimating process and make appropriate changes to improve accuracy. How dependent is your state on volatile revenue sources like income tax revenue in general or capital gains in particular?
- Determine your state's dependency upon jobs from new establishments; ask employers and entrepreneurs what legislators can do to remove barriers to new start-ups.
- Determine the degree to which jobs, taxpayers, and adjusted gross income are lost due to people leaving your state. It's far easier to keep existing customers than to attract new ones.
- Have independent audits of tax subsidy programs to determine their efficacy. Ignore the rosy

return-on-investment estimates produced by government and others who stand to benefit and include unseen consequences in the evaluation. Are the few companies that get a subsidy more likely to create jobs than those that don't? How much economic activity was foregone by raising taxes or fees (or not reducing them) so that money was available for subsidies to a few favored businesses?

Conclusion

Much of what went wrong in Kansas was avoidable, and the undoing of a very good idea—allowing citizens to keep more of their hard-earned money—gets to the crux of the serious state and national challenges we face. The efforts of many elected officials and bureaucrats are not on solving problems in ways that create the best path forward for all Americans to achieve prosperity, but on maintaining and consolidating power.

Kansas conservatives were handed a much larger tax cut than they anticipated but wouldn't structurally balance the budget by reducing the cost of government, even though most would at least privately admit that government was inefficient and spending was out of control. They may not have had enough information at the onset to know exactly where to find the necessary savings, but that issue went largely unaddressed. Asked why the budget wouldn't be balanced by reducing the cost of government, one self-described conservative said, "We'd all lose our jobs if we did that."

The Democrats and Republicans who opposed tax relief still had a fiduciary obligation to balance the budget, but they opposed spending reductions and with one exception didn't propose tax increases until Democrats and moderates gained control of both chambers in 2017. Oh, they spoke passionately to media and constituents about the need to raise taxes, but they didn't want an official legislative record of supporting a tax increase. As explained earlier, Democrats and moderates who denounced the exemption on pass-through income defeated its elimination in 2016; some said they voted against it because it wasn't a big enough tax increase, but even the left-leaning *Wichita Eagle* called them out for not voting their principles. The real reason they kept the exemption was that the public might think the budget challenge was solved and they were counting on citizens' fear and animosity toward conservatives to gain control of the legislature in the 2016 elections.

Public polling proved that citizens didn't want their taxes increased and their number one preference for balancing the budget was to reduce the cost of government, but most elected officials in both parties were determined to impose a huge tax hike on citizens and business, so they ignored public sentiment. Some justified their actions with a classic logical fallacy: "The public voted for me and I want to raise taxes, therefore the public wants a tax increase." But very few candidates clearly said, "Vote for me and I will raise your taxes." Instead, they spoke in vagaries like, "I'm for fiscal responsibility."

Be prepared when candidates come knocking on your door. Instead of listening to "the pitch," hand them your own short questionnaire with pointed questions to ferret their real positions from the obfuscation. ("Do you believe government makes efficient use of my money and couldn't possibly reduce costs without sacrificing quality, and what cuts will you propose if your answer is 'no'?") If you don't get a clear answer, their principles are likely in question.

Getting involved and letting your elected officials know that you intend to hold them accountable may be the only way to ensure that your interests are being represented. As Mahatma Gandhi said, "Be the change you wish to see in the world." It won't be easy and it won't happen overnight, but keep Gandhi's encouragement in mind: "First they ignore you, then they laugh at you, then they fight you, then you win."

But if you want change and don't engage, the future will likely be as described by Yogi Berra: it will be like déjà vu all over again.

Endnotes

1   "Sam Brownback's failed 'experiment' puts state on path to penury." *Washington Post*, September 21, 2014. Accessed May 20, 2017. https://www.washingtonpost.com/opinions/sam-brownbacks-failed-experiment-puts-state-on-path-to-penury/2014/09/21/ded58846-3eb2-11e4-9587-5dafd96295f0_story.html?utm_term=.a45369feb9cd.

2   Kansas Department of Education. Accessed May 20, 2017. http://www.ksde.org/Portals/0/Schoolpercent20Finance/data_warehouse/total_expenditures/d0Stateexp.pdf.

3   *New York Times*, August 5, 2016. Accessed May 20, 2017. https://www.nytimes.com/2016/08/05/opinion/moderation-rears-its-head-in-kansas.html.

4   "FY 2018 Governor's Budget Report" http://budget.ks.gov/publications/FY2018/FY2018_GBR_Vol1--UPDATED--1-12-2017.pdf and "FY 2018 Comparison Report" http://budget.ks.gov/publications/FY2018/FY2018_Comparison_Report--8-4-2017.pdf. Kansas Division of the Budget. Accessed August 14, 2017.

5   Pomerleau, Kyle, Drenkard, Scott and Buhl, John. "What Trump Can Learn From Kansas' Tax Troubles." POLITICO Magazine. May 4, 2017. Accessed May 15, 2017. http://www.politico.com/magazine/story/2017/05/04/what-trump-can-learn-from-kansas-tax-troubles-215103.

6   https://kansaspolicy.org/irs-data-refutes-kansas-tax-evasion-theories/

7   Parkes, Patrick. "Kansas Medicaid Expansion By the Numbers: Is It Really A "Free Lunch?" May 5, 2014. Accessed August 16, 2017. https://kansaspolicy.org/kansas-medicaid-expansion-numbers-really-free-lunch/.

8   Interview with Brandon Smith, Policy Director for Governor Sam Brownback, on August 1, 2017.

9   Horton, Nic, and Jonathan Ingram. "Work Requirements are Working for Kansas Families." July 31, 2017. Accessed August 16, 2017. https://thefga.org/wp-content/uploads/2017/07/Work-Requirements-are-Working-for-Kansas-Families.pdf.

10 https://www.ksrevenue.org/prtaxcredits-LowIncomeStudents.html

11 https://www.kpers.org/pdf/benefitsataglance_kpers3.pdf

12 US Department of Commerce, Bureau of Economic Analysis (BEA). Accessed May 21, 2017. https://www.bea.gov/iTable/iTable.cfm?reqid=70&step=1&isuri=1&acrdn=6#reqid=70&step=1&isuri=1.

13 Ibid.

14 US Census Bureau. US by Legal Form of Organization Tables – 2015. Accessed May 21, 2017. https://www.census.gov/data/tables/2015/econ/cbp/legal-form-organization.html.

15 US Department of Commerce, Bureau of Economic Analysis. SA-25. Accessed May 21, 2017. https://www.bea.gov/iTable/iTable.cfm?reqid=70&step=1&isuri=1&acrdn=6#reqid=70&step=24&isuri=1&7022=4&7023=0&7001=44&7090=70.

16 Bureau of Economic Analysis https://www.bea.gov/regional/docs/msalist.cfm?mlist=5&Display=Display

17 Bureau of Economic Analysis. Accessed October 14, 2017. https://www.bea.gov/iTable/iTable.cfm?reqid=70&step=1&isuri=1&acrdn=7#reqid=70&step=24&isuri=1&7022=11&7023=7&7001=711&7090=70

18   Save Kansas Coalition. June 24, 2016. Accessed May 24, 2017. http://
     d31hzlhk6di2h5.cloudfront.net/20160624/79/ae/87/70/238682375e981de
     0a5a0ed89/GovernorsLtrLink.pdf.
19   The four governors' reigns spanned 1979 to 2008; John Carlin (1979–87), Mike
     Hayden (1987–91), Bill Graves (1995–2003), and Kathleen Sebelius (2003–
     08). Former Governor Joan Finney (1991–95) is deceased. Kathleen Sebelius
     resigned from office in early 2009 to accept a cabinet position in the Obama
     administration.
20   US Department of Commerce, Bureau of Economic Analysis. SA5. Accessed
     May 24, 2017.
21   Ibid.
22   A complete history of all credit rating services actions over the years in
     question wasn't purchased for this review, but Moody's reduced Kansas's credit
     outlook from stable to negative in June 2003: https://www.moodys.com/
     credit-ratings/Kansas-State-of-credit-rating-600028496. A report provided by
     the Kansas Division of the Budget shows Standard & Poor's reduced Kansas's
     credit outlook from stable to negative in August 2002.
23   "Finances: Graves is expected to announce cuts for various agencies." *Topeka
     Capital-Journal*, August 14, 2002. Accessed May 25, 2017. http://cjonline.com/
     stories/081402/kan_bondrating.shtml#.WSdC5usrKM8
24   "Goossen: Set Up for More Financial Trouble." Kansas Center for Economic
     Growth. May 18, 2016. Accessed May 25, 2017. http://realprosperityks.com/
     goossen-set-financial-trouble/.
25   SGF annual spending and tax revenue provided by Kansas Division of the
     Budget.
26   "1993 KPERS Benefit Enhancements and Funding; Attachment A." Kansas
     Public Employees Retirement System.
27   Miliman. Inc. "Kansas Public Employees Retirement System, Valuation Report
     as of December 31, 2009." KPERS.org. December 31, 2009. Accessed May 26,
     2017. https://www.kpers.org/valuationreport123109.pdf.
28   Ibid.
29   "State Pension Plans: Liabilities, Funded Ratios." *Governing* magazine.
     November 29, 2012. Accessed May 26, 2017. http://www.governing.com/
     gov-data/state-pension-funds-retirement-systems-unfunded-liabilities-
     obligations-data.html.
30   Williams, Bob, Jonathan Williams, Ted Lafferty, and Sarah Curry.
     "Unaccountable and Unaffordable 2016: Unfunded Public Pension Liabilities
     Near $5.6 Trillion." American Legislative Exchange Council. October 13, 2016.
     Accessed May 26, 2017. https://www.alec.org/publication/pensiondebt2016/.
31   Ibid.
32   Hall, Arthur P., PhD. "Major Structural Deficits Looming in Kansas." Kansas
     Policy Institute. December 11, 2011. Accessed June 1, 2017. https://kansaspolicy.
     org/major-structural-deficits-looming-kansas/.
33   IRS Migration Data. Accessed May 5, 2017. https://www.irs.gov/uac/
     soi-tax-stats-migration-data
34   Jensen, Nathan M., *Evaluating Firm-Specific Location Incentives: An Application
     to the Kansas PEAK Program* (April 1, 2014). Available at SSRN: https://ssrn.
     com/abstract=2431320 or http://dx.doi.org/10.2139/ssrn.2431320
35   Eveld, Edward, and Diane Stafford. "Kansas Gov. Sam Brownback makes
     'border war' peace offering." April 14, 2016. Accessed August 18, 2017. http://
     www.kansascity.com/news/politics-government/article71869212.html.
36   Ibid.
37   http://www.kslegislature.org/li_2012/b2011_12/measures/documents/supp_
     note_sb196_04_0000.pdf
38   Hall, Arthur P., PhD. *Local Government and the Kansas Productivity Puzzle.*

Lawrence, KS: Center for Applied Economics, University of Kansas School of Business, 2006.

39 "A History of Tax Policy in Kansas" manuscript by The Mercatus Center at George Mason University provided by the author; not yet published as this book went to press.

40 https://governor.kansas.gov/2012-state-of-the-state/. Accessed July 28, 2017.

41 http://www.kslegislature.org/li_2012/b2011_12/measures/sb1/

42 http://www.kslegislature.org/li_2012/b2011_12/measures/documents/supp_note_sb1_04_0000.pdf

43 Ibid.

44 Kobach, Kris. "New Business Formations on the Rise." Kansas Secretary of State. February 8, 2017. Accessed July 16, 2017. http://www.sos.ks.gov/other/news_releases/PR_2017/2016_Business_Formation_Report.pdf.

45 Email from Kathy M. Sachs, deputy assistant secretary of State. Copy in author's possession.

46 Boyes, William, and Stephen Slivinski. "A Thousand Flowers Blooming— Understanding Job Growth and the Kansas Tax Reforms." Kansas Policy Institute. January 2017. Accessed July 16, 2017. For a review of this literature, see Stephen J. Davis, John Haltiwanger, and Ron Jarmin, "Turmoil and Growth: Young Businesses, Economic Churning, and Productivity Gains," Ewing Marion Kauffman Foundation, June 2008, available at: http://www.kauffman.org/~/media/kauffman_org/research%20reports%20and%20covers/2008/06/turmoilandgrowth060208.pdf.

47 Ibid. John Haltiwanger, Ron S. Jarmin, and Javier Miranda. "Who Creates Jobs? Small Versus Large Versus Young," *The Review of Economics and Statistics*, Vol. XCV, No. 2, May 2013, available at: http://www.mitpressjournals.org/doi/pdf/10.1162/REST_a_00288.

48 Hall, Arthur P., PhD. "Embracing Dynamism: The Next Phase in Kansas Economic Development Policy." Center for Applied Economics, University of Kansas School of Business. February 2010. Accessed July 16, 2017. https://www.scribd.com/document/123107020/Embracing-Dynamism-The-Next-Phase-in-Kansas-Economic-Development-Policy.

49 "Kansas Speaks Spring 2017 Statewide Public Opinion Survey." May 2017. Accessed July 16, 2017. https://www.fhsu.edu/uploadedFiles/executive/docking/Kansas%20Speaks%202017(1).pdf.

50 Gleckman, Howard. "What's The Matter With Kansas And Its Tax Cuts? It Can't Do Math." Forbes.com. July 15, 2014. Accessed July 18, 2017. https://www.forbes.com/sites/beltway/2014/07/15/whats-the-matter-with-kansas-and-its-tax-cuts-it-cant-do-math/#6af69d613100.

51 Americans for Tax Reform, accessed August 11, 2017. https://www.atr.org/full-list-ACA-tax-hikes-a6996

52 McMillin, Molly. "End of an era: Boeing in final stages of leaving Wichita." July 29, 2014. Accessed August 11, 2017. http://www.kansas.com/news/business/aviation/article1153168.html.

53 Bureau of Labor Statistics, accessed August 11, 2017. https://www.bls.gov/sae/.

54 Bureau of Economic Analysis, accessed August 11, 2017. https://www.bea.gov/regional/index.htm.

55 US Department of Agriculture, accessed August 24, 2017. https://quickstats.nass.usda.gov/.

56 "2016 ProfitLink Analysis." May 2017. Accessed August 25, 2017. http://www.agmanager.info/kfma/executive-summaries/2016-executive-summary.

57 County sales tax map courtesy of Kansas Department of Revenue, emailed on November 4, 2016.

58 US Energy Information Administration, NYMEX future prices, Cushing OK Crude Future, Henry Hub Natural Gas Spot Price, accessed August 29, 2017. https://www.eia.gov/dnav/pet/hist/LeafHandler.ashx?n=pet&s=rclc1&f=m.

59 US Energy Information Administration, NYMEX future prices, accessed August 29, 2017. https://www.eia.gov/dnav/ng/hist/rngwhhdm.htm.

60 Cross, Edward P. "State of the Oil & Gas Industry—Dynamic Challenges Facing Kansas Oil & Natural Gas Industry." July 2017. Accessed August 26, 2017. http://www.kioga.org/communications/reports/state-of-oil-gas-industry-white-paper-2016/view.

61 Bill description taken from the Supplemental Note on HB 2560 as prepared by Kansas Legislative Research Department at http://www.kslegislature.org/li_2012/b2011_12/measures/documents/supp_note_hb2560_01_0000.pdf and the Fiscal Note prepared for HB 2560 at http://www.kslegislature.org/li_2012/b2011_12/measures/documents/fisc_note_hb2560_00_0000.pdf .

62 Brownback, Sam. 2012 State of the State Address delivered on January, 11, 2012. Accessed on July 12, 2017, from the Lawrence Journal World. http://www2.ljworld.com/news/2012/jan/11/full-text-gov-sam-brownbacks-state-state-address/.

63 Ibid.

64 S Sub for HB 2117 Summary Note. Accessed on July 12, 2017. http://www.kslegislature.org/li_2012/b2011_12/measures/documents/summary_hb_2117_2012.pdf.

65 Cram, Richard. Written testimony to the Kansas Senate Assessment and Taxation Committee. February 14, 2012. http://www.kslegislature.org/li_2012/b2011_12/committees/misc/ctte_s_assess_tax_1_20120214_01_other.pdf.

66 Cooper, Brad, and Davis, Mark. "Brownback's Tax Plan Hits Home with End of Mortgage Deduction," *Kansas City Star*. January 12, 2012. Accessed via *Kansas City Star* archives.

67 Cooper, Brad. "Kansas Gov. Brownback's tax plan would hit poor the hardest." January 18, 2012. http://www.mcclatchydc.com/news/politics-government/article24722452.html.

68 Jordan, Nick. Testimony on HB 2560 before House Tax Committee. February 8, 2012. http://www.kslegislature.org/li_2012/b2011_12/committees/misc/ctte_h_tax_1_20120208_03_other.pdf.

69 Murray, Dan. Testimony on HB 2560 before House Tax Committee. February 8, 2012. http://www.kslegislature.org/li_2012/b2011_12/committees/misc/ctte_h_tax_1_20120208_03_other.pdf.

70 Wareham, Doug. Testimony on HB 2560 before House Tax Committee. February 8, 2012. http://www.kslegislature.org/li_2012/b2011_12/committees/misc/ctte_h_tax_1_20120208_05_other.pdf.

71 Bell, Luke. Testimony on HB 2560 before House Tax Committee. February 9, 2012. http://www.kslegislature.com/li_2012/b2011_12/committees/misc/ctte_h_tax_1_20120209_02_other.pdf.

72 Tallman, Mark. Testimony on HB 2560 before House Tax Committee. February 9, 2012. http://www.kslegislature.com/li_2012/b2011_12/committees/misc/ctte_h_tax_1_20120209_03_other.pdf.

73 Desetti, Mark. Testimony on HB 2560 before House Tax Committee. February 9, 2012. http://www.kslegislature.org/li_2012/b2011_12/committees/misc/ctte_h_tax_1_20120209_04_other.pdf.

74 Eckles. Kent. Testimony on HB 2560 before House Tax Committee. February 8, 2012. http://www.kslegislature.com/li_2012/b2011_12/committees/misc/ctte_h_tax_1_20120208_04_other.pdf.

75 Watkins, Jason. Testimony on HB 2560 before House Tax Committee. February 8, 2012. http://www.kslegislature.org/li_2012/b2011_12/committees/misc/ctte_h_tax_1_20120208_06_other.pdf.

76 Vancrum, Robert. Testimony on HB 2560 before House Tax Committee.

February 8, 2012. http://www.kslegislature.org/li_2012/b2011_12/committees/misc/ctte_h_tax_1_20120208_16_other.pdf.

77 Watkins, Jason. Testimony on HB 2560 before House Tax Committee. February 8, 2012. http://www.kslegislature.org/li_2012/b2011_12/committees/misc/ctte_h_tax_1_20120208_06_other.pdf.

78 Trabert, Dave. Testimony on HB 2560 before House Tax Committee. February 8, 2012. http://www.kslegislature.org/li_2012/b2011_12/committees/misc/ctte_h_tax_1_20120208_09_other.pdf.

79 Ibid.

80 Lauver, Dennis. Testimony before the House Tax Committee. February 8, 2012. http://www.kslegislature.org/li_2012/b2011_12/committees/misc/ctte_h_tax_1_20120208_15_other.pdf.

81 Bangert, Sister Therese, Sisters of Charity testimony on HB 2560 before House Tax Committee, February 8, 2012. http://www.kslegislature.org/li_2012/b2011_12/committees/misc/ctte_h_tax_1_20120209_09_other.pdf.

82 House Tax Committee Sign-in Sheet. February 8, 2017. http://www.kslegislature.com/li_2012/b2011_12/committees/misc/ctte_h_tax_1_20120208_22_other.pdf, and House Tax Committee Sign-in Sheet. February 9, 2017. http://www.kslegislature.org/li_2012/b2011_12/committees/misc/ctte_h_tax_1_20120209_20_other.pdf

83 Eckles, Kent. Kansas Chamber of Commerce Testimony to Senate Assessment and Taxation Committee, February 14, 2012. http://www.kslegislature.com/li_2012/b2011_12/committees/misc/ctte_s_assess_tax_1_20120214_02_other.pdf

84 Tallman, Mark. Testimony on SB 339 before the Senate Assessment and Taxation Committee. February 15, 2012. http://www.kslegislature.com/li_2012/b2011_12/committees/misc/ctte_s_assess_tax_1_20120215_20_other.pdf.

85 Cooper, Brad. "Kansas House Republicans offer their tax plan." *Kansas City Star*. January 20, 2012. Accessed from Kansas City Star archives.

86 Carlson, Richard. Testimony on HB 2747, February 15, 2012. http://www.kslegislature.org/li_2012/b2011_12/committees/misc/ctte_h_tax_1_20120215_01_other.pdf.

87 Cooper, Brad. "Kansas House Republicans offer their tax plan." *Kansas City Star*. January 20, 2012.

88 Kansas Division of Budget Fiscal note. March 7, 2012. http://www.kslegislature.com/li_2012/b2011_12/measures/documents/fisc_note_hb2747_00_0000.pdf.

89 Bell, Luke. Testimony on 2747 before the House Taxation Committee, February 15, 2012. http://www.kslegislature.com/li_2012/b2011_12/committees/misc/ctte_h_tax_1_20120215_02_other.pdf.

90 Rankin, Barbara. Testimony on HB 2747 before House Taxation Committee. February 15, 2012. http://www.kslegislature.org/li_2012/b2011_12/committees/misc/ctte_h_tax_1_20120215_07_other.pdf.

91 Trabert, Dave. Testimony on 2747 before the House Taxation Committee. February 16, 2012. http://www.kslegislature.org/li_2012/b2011_12/committees/misc/ctte_h_tax_1_20120216_01_other.pdf.

92 Vancrum, Robert. Testimony before House Taxation Committee. February 15, 2012. http://www.kslegislature.org/li_2012/b2011_12/committees/misc/ctte_h_tax_1_20120215_08_other.pdf.

93 Pilcher-Cook, Mary. Proposed Amendment to S Sub for HB 2117. http://www.kslegislature.org/li_2012/b2011_12/measures/documents/fa_2012_hb2117_s_5114.pdf .

94 Supplemental Note on S Sub for HB 2117. March 20, 2017. http://www.kslegislature.com/li_2012/b2011_12/measures/documents/supp_note_hb2117_04_0000.pdf.

95 Ibid.

96 Journal of the Senate, pg. 1947. March 21, 2012. http://www.
    kslegislature.com/li_2012/b2011_12/chamber/documents/daily_journal_
    senate_20120322102847.pdf.

97 Kraske, Steve. "Massive tax cuts were the result of Brownback's lie." *Kansas
    City Star.* June 8, 2017. http://www.kansascity.com/opinion/opn-columns-
    blogs/steve-kraske/article155148679.html.

98 Cooper, Brad. "Kansas Senate lines up behind tax cut proposal." *Kansas City
    Star.* March 21, 2012. Accessed from the *Kansas City Star* archives.

99 Ibid.

100 Brownback, Sam. Statement on passage of S Sub for HB 2117. May 9,
    2012. Accessed from https://governor.kansas.gov/governor-brownback-
    tax-reform-will-create-jobs-and-economic-growth/.

101 Shields, Mike. "House poised to vote on compromise tax bill." Kansas Health
    Institute. May 17, 2012. http://www.khi.org/news/article/house-poised-vote-
    compromise-tax-bill.

102 Brownback, Sam. Statement on tax legislation. May 16, 2012. Accessed
    from https://governor.kansas.gov/governor-brownback-supports-tax-
    conference-agreement/.

103 Brownback, Sam. Statement on signing HB 2117. May 18, 2017. Accessed
    from https://governor.kansas.gov/governor-brownback-will-sign-pro-growth-
    tax-legislation.

104 "Chaos in Kansas leads to workable maps." June 11, 2012. Accessed August 27,
    2017. http://www.kansascity.com/opinion/article303936/Chaos-in-Kansas-
    leads-to-workable-maps.html.

105 Hanna, John, and Associated Press. "Victorious on Tuesday, conservative
    Kansas Republicans look to future." November 7, 2012. Accessed August 18,
    2017. http://www.kansascity.com/news/local/article310842/Victorious-on-
    Tuesday-conservative-Kansas-Republicans-look-to-future.html.

106 Trabert, Dave, and Todd Davidson. "States that Spend Less, Tax Less—and
    Grow More." December 14, 2012. Accessed August 27, 2017. https://www.wsj.
    com/articles/SB10001424052970204349404578099233101373940.

107 "2017 Green Book." March 13, 2017. Accessed August 27, 2017. https://
    kansaspolicy.org/2017greenbook/.

108 https://www.youtube.com/watch?v=juDv41jovEA

109 Laffer, Arthur B., Stephen Moore, Rex A. Sinquefield, and Travis H. Brown. *An
    Inquiry into the Nature and Causes of the Wealth of States—How Taxes, Energy,
    and Worker Freedom will Change the Balance of Power Among States.* Hoboken:
    Wiley, 2014.

110 Davidson, Todd, David Tuerck, PhD, Paul Bachman, and Michael Head.
    "Tax Reform Gears Kansas for Growth." July 2012. Accessed August 26, 2017.
    https://kansaspolicy.org/tax-reform-gears-kansas-for-growth/.

111 Sam Brownback. Kansas State of the State Address. Delivered January 15, 2013.
    Accessed on August 4, 2017, from http://www.governing.com/news/state/
    Kansas-brownback-state-of-the-state-speech.html.

112 http://budget.ks.gov/publications/FY2014/FY2014_GBR_Vol1--Corrected_
    1-28-2013.pdf

113 November 2012 Consensus Revenue Estimate http://budget.ks.gov/files/
    FY2014/CRE_Long_Memo_Nov2012.pdf.

114 http://budget.ks.gov/publications/FY2014/FY2014_GBR_Vol1--Corrected_
    1-28-2013.pdf

115 Cooper, Brad. "Kansans' property tax breaks at risk under Brownback plan."
    Kansas City Star. January 23, 2013.

116 Ibid.

117 Parkinson, Mark. 2010 State of the State Address. January 11, 2010. Accessed from
    http://www.ontheissues.org/Archive/2010_State_Mark_Parkinson.htm.

118 Klepper, David. "Kansas Governor calls for higher taxes." *Kansas City Star*. January 12, 2010.

119 Ibid.

120 Morris, Frank. "In Kansas, A 'Glide Path' To No Income Taxes. Will It Work?" NPR *Morning Edition*, February 15, 2013. Accessed August 24, 2017. http://www.npr.org/2013/02/15/171822472/in-kansas-a-glide-path-to-no-income-taxes-will-it-work.

121 Eligon, John. "Kansas' Governor and GOP seek to end income tax." *New York Times*. January 23, 2013. Accessed August 24, 2017 http://www.nytimes.com/2013/01/24/us/politics/gov-sam-brownback-seeks-to-end-kansas-income-tax.html

122 Rothschild, Scott. "Brownback: Keep state sales tax at existing level." *Lawrence Journal World*. January 15, 2013. Accessed August 24, 2017. http://www2.ljworld.com/news/2013/jan/15/brownback-keep-state-sales-tax-current-level-cut-m/.

123 Hanna, John. "Kansas Senate endorses tax package." The Associated Press. February 12, 2013.

124 Cooper, Brad. "Kansas stalemate continues as House defeats tax plan." *Kansas City Star*. May 30, 2013.

125 Hineman, Don. "Don's Legislative update." May 21, 2013. Accessed on August 7, 2017. https://docs.google.com/document/d/1erMvwD24AYRmGVd9iMXjqfoqmDflq9vUpywjmh1YZT4/edit.

126 Cooper, Brad. "Kansas Legislature finally passes tax plan." *Kansas City Star*. June 2, 2013.

127 Editorial. "Bad legislature plagues people of Kansas." *Kansas City Star*, May 31, 2013.

128 Cooper, Brad. "Kansas Legislature finally passes tax plan." *Kansas City Star*. June, 2, 2013.

129 http://www.kslegislature.org/li_2014/b2013_14/measures/documents/summary_hb_2059_2013.pdf

130 Kraske, Steve and Zach Murdock. "Brownback signs Kansas tax measure," June 13, 2013. http://www.kansascity.com/news/local/article321056/Brownback-signs-Kansas-tax-measure.html.

131 Brownback, Sam. 2014 State of the State Address. January 16, 2014. Accessed from http://cjonline.com/news-state/2014-01-16/gov-brownbacks-state-state-address-transcript.

132 Kansas Department of Revenue. January 2014 release. January 31, 2014. https://www.ksrevenue.org/CMS/content//01-31-2014-January-Revenue.pdf.

133 Kansas Department of Revenue. February 2014 release. February 29, 2014. https://www.ksrevenue.org/CMS/content//02-28-2014-February-Revenue.pdf.

134 Kansas Department of Revenue. March 2014 release. March 30, 2014. https://www.ksrevenue.org/CMS/content//03-31-2014-March-Revenue.pdf.

135 Kansas Department of Revenue. April 2014 release. April 30, 2014. https://www.ksrevenue.org/CMS/content//04-30-2014-April-Revenue.pdf.

136 Ibid.

137 Boyd, Donald J., and Lucy Dadayan. "Shortfalls on States' April Tax Returns: Trump Effect, Weak Economy, or Both?" Rockefeller Institute of Government. July 2017. Accessed July 18, 2017.

138 Gleckman, Howard. "What's the Matter with Kansas and Its Tax Cuts? It Can't Do Math." Forbes.com. July 15, 2014. Accessed July 18, 2017.

139 Ibid.

140 "State General Fund Receipts Estimates for FY 2014 and FY 2015." November 8, 2013. Accessed August 18, 2017. http://budget.ks.gov/files/FY2015/CRE_Long_Memo_Nov2013.pdf.

141 "Governor's Consensus Revenue Estimating Working Group Final Recommendations." October 4, 2016. Accessed August 18, 2017. http://budget. ks.gov/files/FY2017/cre_workgroup_report.pdf.

142 Cooper, Brad. "Questions abound as Kansas Legislature adjourns." May 3, 2014. Accessed on August 26, 2017 from http://www.kansascity.com/news/ politics-government/article349303/Questions-abound-as-Kansas-Legislature- adjourns.html.

143 Marso, Andy. "S&P downgrades Kansas bond rating." August 6, 2014. Accessed August 30, 2017. http://cjonline.com/news-state-government- state/2014-08-06/sp-downgrades-kansas-bond-rating.

144 Cooper, Brad. "Moody's downgrades Kansas' credit rating, citing sluggish recovery and risky tax plan." *Kansas City Star*. May 1, 2014. http://www.kansascity.com/news/politics-government/article348210/ Moody%E2%80%99s-downgrades-Kansas%E2%80%99-credit-rating-citing- sluggish-recovery-and-risky-tax-plan.html.

145 "Moody's downgrades Kansas issuer rating to Aa2 from Aa1." April 30, 2014. Accessed September 1, 2017. https://www.moodys.com/research/Moodys- downgrades-Kansas-issuer-rating-to-Aa2-from-Aa1-notched--PR_298383.

146 "Moody's Revises Kansas' Outlook to Negative from Stable." April 6, 2011. Accessed September 1, 2017. https://www.moodys.com/research/ MOODYS-REVISES-KANSAS-OUTLOOK-TO-NEGATIVE-FROM- STABLE-ISSUER-RATING-Rating-Update--RU_16890097.

147 KSN-TV 3 news cast, July 15, 2014. Accessed from https://www.youtube.com/ watch?v=VLGCbVaIY0c.

148 LoGiurato, Brett. "Meet the Republicans who are raising hell over Kansas' 'conservative experiment.'" October 29, 2014. Accessed from http://www. businessinsider.com/kansas-governor-race-brownback-republicans-wint- winter-paul-davis-2014-10.

149 Blumenthal, Paul. "Outside money surge makes Kansas Senate race costliest in state history." Associated Press. October 21, 2014. Accessed from http://www. huffingtonpost.com/2014/10/25/kansas-senate-money_n_6044524.html.

150 Real Clear Politics. https://www.realclearpolitics.com/epolls/2014/senate/ks/ kansas_senate_roberts_vs_orman-5216.html.

151 https://www.ksrevenue.org/CMS/content//01-30-2015-January-Revenue. pdf.

152 https://www.ksrevenue.org/CMS/content//12-31-2014-December-revenue. pdf.

153 Lowry, Bryan. "Budget deficit looms for Sam Brownback, Kansas Legislature as 2015 session begins." *Wichita Eagle*. January 15, 2015. Accessed Aug. 26, 2017. http://www.kansas.com/news/politics-government/article5904450.html.

154 http://www2.ljworld.com/news/2015/jan/15/text-gov-sam-brownbacks- 2015-state-state-address/

155 Kansas Budget Memorandum. FY 2015 State General Fund Allotment. December 9, 2014. http://media.khi.org/news/documents/2014/12/09/Allotment_ Letters_Plan--12-09-2014.pdf.

156 Lowry, Bryan. "As Gov. Brownback signs Kansas budget plan, he denies it's a tax increase." *Wichita Eagle*. June 16, 2016. Accessed from http://www. kansascity.com/news/politics-government/article24643096.html.

157 Ibid.

158 Brownback, Sam. 2015 State of the State Address. January 15, 2015. http:// www2.ljworld.com/news/2015/jan/15/text-gov-sam-brownbacks-2015-state- state-address/.

159 Kansas 2017 Budget Director Presentation. Kansas Division of Budget. January 11, 2017. http://budget.ks.gov/publications/FY2018/FY2018_Budget_ Overview--01-11-2017.pdf

160 Ibid.

161 Brownback, Sam. 2015 State of the State Address. January 15, 2015. http://www2.
ljworld.com/news/2015/jan/15/text-gov-sam-brownbacks-2015-state-state-
address/

162 Ibid.

163 Ibid.

164 Davis, Miranda and Woodall, Hunter. "Finance legislation passes keeping
schools open." *Kansas City Star*. June 24, 2016. http://www.kansascity.com/
news/state/kansas/article85773397.html.

165 Alvarez & Marsal State Efficiency Study http://www.kslegresearch.org/
KLRD-web/Publications/AppropriationsRevenue/KansasStatewideEfficiency
InterimRpt2016Jan12.pdf.

166 http://www.kansas.com/news/politics-government/article54279820.html.

167 Rose, Steve. "Assessment is bleak for sorry state of Kansas economy." *Kansas
City Star*. February 20, 2016. Accessed from http://www.kansascity.com/
opinion/opn-columns-blogs/steve-rose/article61369767.html on August 26,
2017.

168 Denning, Jim. Written testimony. April 28, 2016. http://www.kslegislature.
org/li_2016/b2015_16/committees/ctte_s_assess_tax_1/documents/
testimony/20160428_01.pdf.

169 Smith, Greg. Written testimony. http://www.kslegislature.org/li_2016/
b2015_16/committees/ctte_s_assess_tax_1/documents/testimony/20160428_
22.pdf.

170 Montgomery, Rick. "They get tax breaks, and 'they feel like freeloaders.'"
Kansas City Star. August 28, 2016. http://www.kansascity.com/news/politics-
government/article98185532.html.

171 Email exchange dated May 19, 2017. Copy in author's possession.

172 Internal Revenue Service Tax Stats. Accessed May 20, 2017. https://www.irs.gov/
uac/soi-tax-stats-historic-table-2.

173 Kansas Department of Revenue, "Kansas Tax Policy and Economy Review"
(July 2016).

174 Historic data attached to email dated March 14, 2017. Copy in author's
possession.

175 DeBacker, Jason Matthew and Heim, Bradley and Ramnath, Shanthi and Ross,
Justin M., *The Impact of State Taxes on Pass-Through Businesses: Evidence from
the 2012 Kansas Income Tax Reform* (July 2016). Available at SSRN: https://
ssrn.com/abstract=2958353.

176 Herbert, Danedri. "Statistical Noise Crowds Kansas Tax Reform Study
Findings." *Sentinel*. May 1, 2017. Accessed May 16, 2017. https://sentinelksmo.
org/statistical-noise-crowds-kansas-tax-reform-study-findings/.

177 Brownlee, Phillip. "Democrats, GOP moderates wimp out on tax votes."
Wichita Eagle. May 4, 2016. Accessed on September 3, 2017. http://www.
kansas.com/opinion/editorials/article75434617.html

178 Lowry, Bryan. "Kansas House rejects bill to roll back tax exemption for
business owners." April 29, 2016, www.kansas.com/news/politics-government/
article74661562.html. Accessed Sept. 3, 2017.

179 Ibid.

180 Llopis-Jepsen, Celia. "Kansas lawmakers continue hunt for tax solution."
May 4, 2017. Accessed September 3, 2017. http://cjonline.com/news/
state-government/2017-05-04/kansas-lawmakers-continue-hunt-tax-
solution.

181 http://www.kshb.com/news/local-news/kansas-legislature-changes-as-more-
democrats-win

182 "Kansas Freedom Index." July 2017. Accessed August 25, 2017. https://
kansaspolicy.org/freedom-index/.

183 Franko, James. "Legislature Moves Away from Freedom in 2017 Session." July 7, 2017. Accessed August 25, 2017. https://kansaspolicy.org/away-from-freedom-2017-session/.

184 Email correspondence with Kansas Division of the Budget; copy in author's possession.

185 "Kansas Speaks Spring 2017 Statewide Public Opinion Survey." May 2017. Accessed July 16, 2017. https://www.fhsu.edu/uploadedFiles/executive/docking/Kansas%20Speaks%202017(1).pdf.

186 The Kansas Chamber. May 31, 2017. Accessed July 16, 2017. http://www.kansaschamber.org/news/2017/05/31/kansas-voters-poll.

187 Kansas Policy Institute. February 8, 2017. Accessed July 16, 2017. http://www.surveyusa.com/client/PollReport.aspx?g=8950f239-20cc-416d-9aec-23803815c668.

188 "2017 Green Book." Kansas Policy Institute. Accessed July 13, 2017. https://kansaspolicy.org/2017greenbook/.

189 https://governor.kansas.gov/wp-content/uploads/2017/01/2017-State-of-the-State.pdf

190 http://www.kslegislature.org/li/b2017_18/measures/sb188/

191 http://www.kslegislature.org/li/b2017_18/measures/hb2178/

192 Woodall, Hunter. "Brownback tax cut on chopping block if bill continues to advance in Kansas House." February 15, 2017. Accessed August 25, 2017. http://www.kansascity.com/news/politics-government/article132904444.html.

193 Salazar, Daniel. "Kansas Senate sends income tax increase to the governor." February 17, 2017. Accessed August 25, 2017. http://www.kansas.com/news/politics-government/article133321784.html.

194 http://www.kslegislature.org/li/b2017_18/measures/documents/hb2178_enrolled.pdf

195 https://www.youtube.com/watch?v=2XYbyklJb2M

196 Brownback, Sam. Statement on SB 214. April 5, 2017. Accessed from https://governor.kansas.gov/governor-sam-brownback-issues-statement-on-sb-214/.

197 Shorman, Jonathan. "Flat tax would offer victory to Brownback, but lawmakers skeptical." 5 Apr. 2017, www.kansas.com/news/politics-government/article142977444.html. Accessed 26 Aug. 2017.

198 Shorman, Jonathan. "Flat tax would offer victory to Brownback, but lawmakers skeptical." April 5, 2017, www.kansas.com/news/politics-government/article142977444.html. Accessed August 26, 2017.

199 http://www.kslegislature.org/li/b2017_18/measures/documents/hb2395_01_0000.pdf

200 https://www.kansastruthcaucus.org/single-post/2017/05/22/Legislators-Unveil-Republican-Balanced-Budget-Solution

201 "2015 Public Elementary-Secondary Education Finance Data." June 14, 2017. Accessed August 26, 2017. https://www.census.gov/data/tables/2015/econ/school-finances/secondary-education-finance.html.

202 Actual amounts for school years 2010 through 2017 at http://datacentral.ksde.org/school_finance_reports.aspx and the 2018 estimate was provided by KSDE Deputy Commissioner Dale Dennis in an email dated November 8, 2016; copy in author's possession.

203 Trabert, Dave. "Kansas School Funding Set New Records in 2017," November 6, 2017. Accessed December 9, 2017. https://kansaspolicy.org/kansas-school-funding-set-new-records-2017/.

204 http://www.kslegislature.org/li/b2017_18/measures/documents/hb2142_00_0000.pdf

205 http://underthedomeks.org/category/advocacy-action/page/9/

206 http://www.kslegislature.org/li/b2017_18/measures/documents/hb2143_00_0000.pdf

207 http://www.kslegislature.org/li/b2017_18/committees/ctte_h_k12_education_budget_1/documents/testimony/20170201_05.pdf

208 Travis, Jess. Testimony on HB 2143. Accessed from http://www.kslegislature.com/li/b2017_18/committees/ctte_h_k12_education_budget_1/documents/testimony/20170201_08.pdf.

209 Hutchinson, John. Testimony on HB 2143 Accessed from http://www.kslegislature.com/li/b2017_18/committees/ctte_h_k12_education_budget_1/documents/testimony/20170201_09.pdf.

210 Muci, Darren. Testimony on HB 2143. Accessed from http://www.kslegislature.com/li/b2017_18/committees/ctte_h_k12_education_budget_1/documents/testimony/20170201_06.pdf.

211 http://www.kslegislature.org/li/b2017_18/committees/ctte_h_k12_education_budget_1/documents/testimony/20170201_07.pdf

212 http://www.kslegislature.org/li/b2017_18/committees/ctte_h_k12_education_budget_1/documents/testimony/20170201_12.pdf

213 http://www.kslegislature.org/li/b2017_18/committees/ctte_h_k12_education_budget_1/documents/testimony/20170201_15.pdf

214 The analysis shown at https://kansaspolicy.org/tax-change-recap/ was emailed by Kansas Legislative Research Department.

215 Lowry, Bryan, and Hunter Woodall. "Brownback saw political advantage for him in veto override, GOP lawmakers say." June 15, 2017. Accessed August 26, 2017. http://www.kansascity.com/news/politics-government/article156301214.html#0.

216 Haughton, Laurence. *It's Not What You Say . . . It's What You Do*. Doubleday, 2004. http://www.laurencehaughton.com/books/page.php?content=book.

217 Ibid, page 107. The author credits Anand Sharma of TBD Consulting Group for the CAVE acronym.

218 https://www.alec.org/model-policy/statement-alec-principles-of-taxation/

219 Ries, Al, and Jack Trout. *Positioning: Winning the Battle for Your Mind*; Twentieth Anniversary Edition. McGraw Hill, 2001.

220 Kjar, Kevan, and Kelly Shaw. *The Arrowhead: Winning the Story War*. Eagle, ID: ArrowHead[3] Consulting, 2011. http://arrowhead3.com/home/.

221 Ibid.

222 Trabert, Dave, "Death of a (Policy) Salesman." State Policy Network, January/February issue of SPN Magazine.

223 Based on review of weekly agendas for House Appropriations at http://www.kslegislature.org/li/b2017_18/committees/ctte_h_apprprtns_1/documents/ and Senate Ways and Means at http://www.kslegislature.org/li/b2017_18/committees/ctte_s_wam_1/.

224 *State Budget Reform Toolkit*. American Legislative Exchange Council (ALEC), October 11, 2011. https://www.alec.org/publication/state-budget-reform-toolkit/.

225 Anderson, Steve, and Patrick Parkes. "A Legislator's Guide to Delivering Better Service at a Better Price." Kansas Policy Institute, July 2014. https://kansaspolicy.org/kpi-paper-a-legislators-budget-guide/.

226 Kansas Legislative Research Department, accessed August 9, 2017 at http://www.kslegresearch.org/KLRD-web/PerformanceBasedBudgeting.html.

227 K.S.A. 79-3620(c)(6) http://www.kslegislature.org/li/b2017_18/statute/079_000_0000_chapter/079_036_0000_article/079_036_0020_section/079_036_0020_k/ and K.S.A. 79-3710(c)(6) http://www.kslegislature.org/li/b2017_18/statute/079_000_0000_chapter/079_037_0000_article/079_037_0010_section/079_037_0010_k/

About the Authors

Dave Trabert is President of Kansas Policy Institute, where he also does research and writes on fiscal policy and education issues. His published work includes "A Five-Year Budget Plan for the State of Kansas," "Student-Focused Funding Solutions for Public Education," "Removing Barriers to Better Public Education," "A Historical Perspective of State Aid, Tuition and Spending for State Universities in Kansas," and "Volume III: Analysis of K–12 Spending in Kansas," a primer on K–12 finance.

Trabert regularly testifies before Kansas House and Senate committees on state budget, tax, and education issues and was an appointed member of the Kansas K–12 Student Achievement and Efficiency Commission. He currently serves on the Tax and Fiscal Policy Task Force and co-chairs the Education Finance Joint Working Group for the American Legislative Exchange Council.

His commentaries have been published by *The Wall Street Journal*, *Investor's Business Daily*, *Forbes*, *Washington Times*, *Washington Examiner*, TheHill.com and The Daily Caller. His guest editorials have also been published in many Kansas newspapers, including the *Wichita Eagle*, *Topeka Capital-Journal*, *Hays Daily News*, *Kansas City Star*, *Hutchinson News*, and the *Manhattan Free Press*.

He graduated cum laude from West Liberty University with a degree in Business Administration.

Danedri Herbert is an editor for *The Sentinel*, an online news service (SentinelKSMO.com) dedicated to holding media and government accountable. Previously, she was an editor and reporter for *Gardner News* and a columnist for the *Kansas City Star*. Her work has also appeared in the *Kansas City Star*, the *Hutchinson News*, *Budget and Tax News*, and *K-Stater Magazine*. She once won a competition for being the most average person and is listed in Kevin O'Keefe's book *The Average American: The Extraordinary Search for the Nation's Most Ordinary Citizen*. Herbert graduated from Kansas State University with a degree in journalism. She and her husband live in Kansas with their deaf dog, Keller.

Acknowledgments

This book would not have been possible without the assistance, advice, and participation of many people, especially those listed below. My heartfelt gratitude goes to:

Kansas Policy Institute Vice President/Policy Director **James Franko**, who birthed the idea to tell this important story.

My co-author, **Danedri Herbert**, for her friendship, enthusiasm, and dogged determination to complete the project on schedule, and to **Amy Hayden**, for encouraging Danedri every day.

Kansas Policy Institute **trustees, advisors, and generous donors** who underwrote publishing the book, making it possible to send a complimentary copy to every state legislator in the United States. And to the **Heartland Institute**, for assisting with the national distribution to state legislators.

Authors **Laurence Haughton** and **Kevan Kjar**, for sharing their expertise in building and executing successful strategies.

David W. Gibson and his son, **Dave Gibson**, who helped explain the vagaries of farm commodity prices, and to the Kansas Independent Oil and Gas Association, particularly KIOGA President **Edward Cross** and Past President **Nick Powell**, for their insight into the oil and gas industry.

The Kansas Department of Revenue provided a tremendous amount of data and insight over the last few years; special thanks goes to KDOR Secretary **Sam Williams**, **Kathleen Smith**, **Michael Austin**, **Justin Carroll**, **Steve Stotts**, and former Secretary **Nick Jordan**. State Budget Director **Shawn Sullivan**, Kansas Legislative Research Department Assistant Director for Fiscal Affairs **J. G. Scott**, and former State Budget Director **Steve Anderson** also generously shared their expertise.

Special thanks also to the American Legislative Exchange Council (ALEC), including Chief Economist **Jonathan Williams**, and Tax & Fiscal Policy Task Force Executive Director **Joel Griffith**, for tirelessly telling the true story of the Kansas tax-relief effort to legislators and media across the country.

And last but not least, to my family and my wonderful fiancée, Pam, for their encouragement and indulgence of my passion for liberty.

You Can Help Tell Americans About Controlling Taxing and Spending in Your State

This path-breaking book first defines the problem of taxing and spending at the state level and then offers a way out—before it is too late. Many other states have succeeded in cutting taxes and spending. The failure of the Kansas tax cuts and reforms offer as many valuable lessons as do the many successes elsewhere. Please order copies for your state legislator, your local activist friends, and your local media.

Special Bulk Copy Discount Schedule

1 book $12.95	25 books $ 95.00	500 books $1,250.00
5 books $25.00	50 books $175.00	1000 books $1,850.00
10 books $45.00	100 books $325.00	

All prices include postage and handling.

- - - - - - - - - - - - - - -

JAMESON BOOKS, INC   **ORDER TOLL FREE**
Post Office Box 738   **(800) 426-1357**
Ottawa, IL 61350

Please send me _____ copies of *What Was* Really *the Matter with the Kansas Tax Plan*

Enclosed is my check for $ _____ or please charge my
❏ MasterCard   ❏ Visa   ❏ Amex   ❏ Discover card,

No._____ Exp. Date _____

Signature_____ Telephone _____

Name_____

Address_____

City_____ State_____ Zip_____

Illinois residents please add 6.5% sales tax. Please allow 2 weeks for delivery.